THE A

WITH

CAPRI, NAPLES &

POMPEII

TRAVEL GUIDE 2024-2025

Unveiling Adventures, Culinary Delights, Rich
History, Cozy Accommodation and Hidden
Gems

Alex Fowler

TABLE OF CONTENTS

INTRODUCTION

Prepare to be swept away by the vibrant colors, captivating charm, and breathtaking beauty of the Amalfi Coast and Capri. Tucked away on Italy's southern shores, this enchanting destination unfolds like a painting come to life. Imagine cascading cliffs adorned with pastel-hued villages, their windows basking in the golden glow of the Mediterranean sun. Picture yourself wandering through maze-like alleyways, the scent of lemon blossoms and freshly baked bread dancing in the air. The turquoise waters of the Tyrrhenian Sea sparkle, beckoning you to dive into hidden coves and glide past rugged coastlines.

But the Amalfi Coast and Capri offer more than just postcard-perfect scenery. Delve into a rich tapestry of history, where ancient ruins whisper tales of Roman emperors and legendary sirens. Savor the vibrant culture, where colorful festivals erupt in the piazzas and the rhythm of life dances to the strumming of mandolins. Indulge in a culinary adventure, where fresh seafood melts on your tongue, and locally grown lemons infuse every dish with a burst of sunshine.

Whether you're a seasoned traveler or a wide-eyed adventurer, the Amalfi Coast and Capri promise an unforgettable experience. This guide is your key to unlocking its treasures. We'll guide you through picturesque villages, from Positano's cliffside haven to Ravello's terraced paradise. We'll take you on a journey to Capri, where the glamorous piazzas mingle with secluded coves and the Blue Grotto paints the sea with an ethereal glow. We'll introduce you to the vibrant energy of Naples, where art and history collide in a whirlwind of passion. And we'll even transport you back in time, exploring the awe-inspiring ruins of Pompeii, frozen in time by volcanic ash.

So, pack your sense of wonder, your appetite for adventure, and your swimsuit for days soaking up the sun. This guide is your invitation to paint your own masterpiece on the canvas of the Amalfi Coast and Capri. Let's dive in and discover the magic together!

Overview of the Amalfi Coast

Imagine a place where the sea dances against rugged cliffs, colorful houses tumble down verdant slopes, and every turn reveals a breathtaking vista. This isn't just a painting it's the Amalfi Coast, a jewel clinging to the southern shores of Italy, waiting to captivate your senses.

More than just a string of seaside towns, the Amalfi Coast is a tapestry woven from history, culture, and natural splendor. Its story stretches back to ancient times, whispering tales of Roman emperors and maritime adventures. The air vibrates with the spirit of artists and poets who found inspiration in its cliffs and coves. And amidst the vibrant piazzas and charming alleyways, the warmth of Italian hospitality welcomes you with open arms.

This 30-mile stretch of coastline unfurls like a visual symphony. Pastel-hued houses, adorned with cascading bougainvillea, cling precariously to cliffs that plunge into the turquoise embrace of the

Tyrrhenian Sea. Winding roads snake through terraced vineyards and lemon groves, offering glimpses of hidden coves and secluded beaches. Each village boasts its own unique charm, from the cliffside haven of Positano to the terraced paradise of Ravello, from the bustling Amalfi with its Duomo's grandeur to the quaint fishing village of Cetara.

But the Amalfi Coast is more than just a feast for the eyes. Every corner hums with life. The scent of freshly baked bread and blooming citrus mingles with the salty air. Boats bob in picturesque harbors, ready to whisk you away to hidden coves and secluded beaches. On cobbled piazzas, the rhythm of life dances to the strumming of mandolins and the chatter of animated conversations. And when the sun dips below the horizon, the sky ignites with a fiery symphony of color, leaving you breathless with its beauty.

This is not just a place to visit it's an experience to be savored. Here, you can hike along cliffside trails, their panoramas taking your breath away. You can dive into the crystal-clear waters, exploring secret coves and vibrant coral reefs. You can indulge in culinary delights, from fresh seafood plucked straight from the sea to pasta infused with the sunshine of lemon groves. You can immerse yourself in ancient history, walking in the footsteps of emperors and gladiators. And you can simply relax, basking on sun-drenched beaches and letting the rhythm of the waves lull you into a state of pure bliss. So, dear traveler, pack your sense of wonder, your appetite for adventure, and your swimsuit for days soaking up the sun. The Amalfi Coast awaits, ready to weave its magic around you. Come, discover its hidden treasures, embrace its vibrant spirit, and create memories that will last a lifetime.

Unique features and attractions

While the Amalfi Coast's postcard-perfect beauty can leave you speechless, its allure extends far beyond stunning cliffs and charming villages. This treasure trove of unique experiences and hidden gems invites you to delve deeper and discover its soul. Here are just a few highlights that set the Amalfi Coast apart:

1. A Cliffside Wonderland

Path of the Gods: Hike this legendary trail between Agerola and Nocelle, where breathtaking panoramas unfold with every step. Imagine weaving through ancient forests, perched precariously above the turquoise sea, and feeling history whisper from the ruins of Roman aqueducts.

Fiordo di Furore: Witness nature's artistic masterpiece, a fjord carved into towering cliffs, accessible only by foot or boat. Kayak through a tunnel under the village, marveling at waterfalls cascading into the emerald water, and soak in the serene atmosphere.

Villa Cimbrone: Explore this breathtaking estate in Ravello, where manicured gardens bloom with exotic flora, statues tell mythological tales, and the Terrace of Infinity seems to suspend you between sky and sea.

2. A Cultural Tapestry

Amalfi Duomo: Step into a symphony of Byzantine and Romanesque architecture, featuring a majestic bell tower and dazzling mosaics. Imagine the whispers of centuries echoing within, and let the beauty transport you to a bygone era.

- avello Festival: Immerse yourself in the vibrant energy of this summer festival, where classical music fills the air, renowned artists showcase their talents, and the town transforms into a stage for cultural celebration.

- **Limonecello Ceremony:** Witness the traditional production of this iconic liquor in Maiori, with lemon peels dancing in giant vats under the warm southern sun. Sample the freshly made elixir, and savor the taste of Amalfi's sunshine.

3. A Feast for the Senses
- **Cooking Class in Conca dei Marini:** Learn the secrets of Amalfitan cuisine from a local expert, mastering fresh seafood dishes, fragrant pasta sauces, and decadent desserts. Indulge in your creations with panoramic views of the sea, feeling the warmth of Italian hospitality.

- **Wine Tasting in Tramonti:** Discover the hidden gem of Tramonti, a haven for artisanal winemakers. Sip on locally produced varietals amidst rolling vineyards, and let the taste of the land tell you its story.

- **Boat Tour to Emerald Grotto:** Glide through hidden coves, past craggy cliffs, and into the magical Emerald Grotto. Watch as sunlight filters through the water, bathing the cave in an ethereal emerald glow, a sight to remember forever.

4. An Adventure Playground

- **Kayaking the Coastline:** Explore hidden coves, secret beaches, and dramatic rock formations from the water's perspective. Paddle your way through turquoise waters, feeling the rhythm of the waves, and discover the coast's hidden beauty.

- **Scuba Diving in the Marine Reserve:** Dive into a vibrant underwater world teeming with colorful fish, coral reefs, and ancient shipwrecks. Explore marine life hidden beneath the surface, and feel the thrill of underwater adventure.

- **Paragliding over Praiano:** Soar through the sky, feeling the wind beneath your wings, and witness the Amalfi Coast's breathtaking panorama from a bird's-eye view. Experience the unparalleled thrill of flight and create memories that will last a lifetime.

CHAPTER 1

Planning Your Trip

Welcome, adventurer! Before you plunge into the dazzling azure waters and vibrant piazzas of the Amalfi Coast, let's weave the tapestry of your perfect Italian escape. This chapter is your personal travel alchemist, transforming wishes into itineraries, worries into whispers, and logistics into smooth sailing.

When to Paint Your Amalfi Masterpiece

Spring's gentle brushstrokes: Blossoming landscapes, fewer crowds, and budget-friendly deals paint a delightful picture. Imagine wildflowers cascading down cliffs and the air abuzz with anticipation.

Summer's vibrant palette: Sun-kissed beaches, buzzing nightlife, and a contagious energy reign supreme. Dive into the turquoise waters, savor gelato under starry skies, and dance to the rhythm of life.

Autumn's golden whispers: Cooler temperatures, harvest festivals, and breathtaking foliage offer a serene escape. Hike through vineyards bursting with grapes, indulge in culinary delights, and embrace the quiet contemplation.

Winter's cozy charm: Christmas markets, fewer crowds, and lower prices bring a unique, romantic touch. Snuggle up in charming cafes, explore historic towns, and witness the festive spirit.

Getting There – Your Gateway to Paradise

Naples Capodichino Airport: The closest and most affordable option, perfect for exploring Naples and Sorrento. Public transportation or private transfers make for a smooth transition.

Rome Fiumicino Airport: A larger hub with more international connections, but requires additional travel time to reach the Amalfi Coast. High-speed trains or private transfers are your allies.

Finding Your Amalfi Abode

Cliffside havens: Luxurious hotels offering breathtaking views and exclusive access to the sea. Perfect for honeymooners and luxury seekers.

Charming guesthouses: Family-run gems tucked away in quaint villages. Experience local warmth and authenticity at budget-friendly prices.

Beachfront retreats: Wake up to the sound of waves and enjoy direct access to the sandy shores. Ideal for families and water enthusiasts.

Agriturismos: Immerse yourself in rural life in charming farmhouses amidst rolling hills and lemon groves. Ideal for nature lovers and foodies.

Fueling Your Amalfi Adventures

Fresh seafood feasts: Dive into plates of glistening fish, pasta with local catches, and succulent pizza baked in wood-fired ovens. Budget-friendly trattorias and Michelin-starred restaurants cater to every palate.

Liquid sunshine: Limoncello, the Amalfi Coast's liquid gold, awaits in charming cafes and vibrant bars. Don't miss local wines, craft beers, and refreshing spritzes.

Picnics under the sun: Pack fresh mozzarella, juicy tomatoes, crusty bread, and local fruits for the ultimate gourmet escape. Find a secluded cove or a sun-drenched piazza and savor the flavors of la dolce vita.

Staying Safe & Healthy

- Travel insurance ensures peace of mind.
- Pack sunscreen, a hat, and comfortable walking shoes.

- Familiarize yourself with local scams and safety tips.
- Learn basic Italian phrases to enhance your experience.

Money & Visas
- Euros are the currency. ATMs are readily available, but carrying some cash is recommended.
- Visa requirements vary depending on your nationality. Check with your local embassy or consulate.

Cultural Do's & Don'ts
- Dress modestly when visiting churches and religious sites.
- Learn basic Italian greetings and polite phrases.
- Respect local customs and traditions.
- Tipping is not expected, but appreciated for good service.

When to Go

Choosing the right time for your visit is like selecting the perfect brushstroke for your Italian masterpiece – it dictates the colors, the mood, and the overall experience. So, let's explore the unique flavors of each season and find the one that sings to your soul!

Spring's Gentle Brushstrokes (April-May)

- Imagine pastel hues painting the landscape as wildflowers cascade down cliffs and ancient ruins bask in the mild sunshine.
- The crowds are still few and far between, offering tranquility and budget-friendly deals.
- Hikes along coastal paths are delightful, and the water is warming up for early dips.
- Local festivals and Easter celebrations add a vibrant touch to the air.

Summer's Vibrant Palette (June-August)

- Sun-kissed beaches become your playground, inviting you to dive into the turquoise waters and bask in the golden rays.
- Nightlife buzzes in lively piazzas, and the energy is contagious as gelato drips down chins and laughter fills the air.
- Expect larger crowds and higher prices, but the atmosphere is one of pure joie de vivre.
- Boat trips to hidden coves and bustling markets add a dose of adventure and cultural immersion.

Autumn's   Golden   Whispers (September-October)

- The landscapes transform into a riot of gold and red, offering breathtaking hikes through vineyards bursting with grapes.
- Cooler temperatures provide a respite from the summer heat, making exploration a comfortable pleasure.

- The harvest festivals bring a sense of tradition and delicious aromas of local specialties.
- Prices start to dip, and crowds thin out, offering a relaxed and authentic experience.

Winter's Cozy Charm (November-March)
- Christmas markets twinkle in piazzas, transforming the coast into a wonderland of festive cheer.
- Hotels offer tempting deals, and crowds are minimal, allowing you to explore at your own pace.
- Cozy cafes become havens for hot chocolate and limoncello, while historic towns reveal their ancient secrets.
- While swimming in the sea might not be on the agenda, charming walks and cultural discoveries abound.

Remember, the "perfect" season depends on your personal preferences:

Sun worshippers: Summer's warmth and beach bliss are your calling.

Budget travelers: Spring and autumn offer lower prices and fewer crowds.

Nature lovers: Spring's wildflowers and autumn's foliage paint stunning landscapes.

Culinary adventurers: Harvest festivals in autumn and fresh seafood all year round beckon.

Romance seekers: Winter's quiet charm and Christmas magic create a special ambiance.

Getting There

Your Amalfi Coast adventure begins the moment you embark on your journey, and choosing the right way to arrive sets the tone for your Italian escape. But fear not, dear traveler, for this chapter is your compass, guiding you through the transportation options to reach this sun-drenched haven.

Naples Capodichino Airport: Your closest gateway to paradise, Naples Capodichino is perfect for exploring Naples itself and seamlessly transitioning to the Amalfi Coast. Budget-friendly flights and quick transfers by bus, train, or private car make it a top choice. Imagine hopping off the plane and being whisked away through vibrant Naples streets, anticipation brewing with every twist and turn.

Rome Fiumicino Airport: A larger hub with more international connections, Rome Fiumicino offers global convenience but adds a bit more travel time. High-speed trains whisk you along scenic countryside, revealing glimpses of rolling hills and ancient ruins before depositing you at your Amalfi Coast destination. Think of it as an extended appetizer to your Italian feast, each mile showcasing the country's beauty.

Cruising into Paradise: Feeling the gentle sway of the ocean beneath your feet is a unique way to arrive. Cruise ships dock in Sorrento or Salerno, offering breathtaking coastal views and the chance to explore other Mediterranean gems before immersing yourself in the Amalfi Coast's charm. Picture yourself sipping cocktails on deck, the salty breeze carrying the promise of sun-kissed beaches and vibrant piazzas.

Driving the Amalfi Dream: For independent spirits, renting a car and navigating the winding coastal roads can be an exhilarating experience. Imagine feeling the wind in your hair as you hug cliffside curves, the sea sparkling below like a sapphire ribbon. However, be prepared for narrow roads, limited parking, and potentially high rental costs during peak season.

No matter your arrival style, let's unravel the details:

- **Naples Capodichino:** Public bus (€5-10), train (€10-20), private transfer (from €60).
- **Rome Fiumicino Airport:** High-speed train (€40-70), private transfer (from €150).
- **Cruises:** Varies depending on itinerary and cruise line.
- **Car rental:** Prices vary depending on season and car type. Consider parking challenges and traffic, especially during peak season.

Remember, the perfect arrival option depends on your priorities. Budget travelers might favor Naples Capodichino, while time-pressed adventurers might choose Rome Fiumicino. For a luxurious touch, consider a cruise, and for independent souls, the thrill of the open road beckons.

Money & Visas

This chapter is your financial compass, guiding you through the currency, visa requirements, and budgeting tips to ensure your Italian escape is smooth sailing (or should we say, smooth strolling?).

Currency Confusion? Conquering Euros!

- The official currency of Italy is the Euro (€).
- ATMs are readily available throughout the Amalfi Coast, especially in towns and larger villages.
- Carrying some cash is recommended for smaller shops, cafes, and unexpected gelato cravings.
- Credit cards are widely accepted, but some smaller establishments might have minimum spending requirements.

- Tipping is not expected, but a small gesture of appreciation for good service is always welcome.

Visa Voyage: Unlocking the Italian Door
- Most visitors from North America, Australia, New Zealand, and many European countries can stay in Italy for up to 90 days within a 180-day period without a visa.
- Check with your local embassy or consulate for specific visa requirements based on your nationality and length of stay.
- If you plan to stay longer than 90 days, apply for the appropriate visa in advance.

Budgeting Bliss: Crafting Your Amalfi Spending Masterpiece

Accommodation: Prices vary greatly depending on location, season, and hotel type.

Food: Budget for an average of €20-40 per person for a meal, with trattorias being more affordable than Michelin-starred restaurants.

Activities: Entrance fees for museums and archaeological sites can range from €5-20.

Transportation: Public transportation is affordable, while private transfers and boat tours can be pricier.

Souvenirs: Local ceramics, limoncello, and handcrafted goods make charming mementos, but be mindful of your budget.

Pro Tips for Financial Savvy
- Travel during the shoulder seasons (spring and autumn) for better deals on flights and accommodation.
- Take advantage of city passes for discounted entry to multiple attractions.
- Pack snacks and drinks for picnics on the beach or in scenic spots.

- Consider utilizing public transportation instead of taxis whenever possible.
- Ask locals for recommendations on budget-friendly restaurants and experiences.

Remember, your Amalfi Coast adventure can be tailored to your financial comfort zone. So, whether you're a backpacker seeking budget-friendly thrills or a luxury traveler embracing la dolce vita, this chapter equips you with the knowledge and tips to navigate the financial side of your Italian escape.

CHAPTER 2

Getting Around

This chapter is your transportation compass, guiding you through the diverse options to conquer the cliffs and explore every charming corner of this Italian paradise.

Buses: Your Affordable All-Terrain Ally

- Hop on the vibrant blue SITA buses for a budget-friendly, efficient way to travel between major towns and villages.
- Enjoy panoramic views from your window seat as the road snakes along the cliffs, offering glimpses of hidden coves and picturesque harbors.
- Tickets are affordable (around €2-5) and readily available at local newsstands, bars, or on the bus itself.
- Be prepared for potential crowds during peak season and limited schedules in smaller villages.

Ferries: Embracing the Azure Pathway
- Glide across the sparkling Mediterranean on a ferry, admiring the dramatic coastline from a different perspective.
- Hop between Sorrento, Amalfi, Capri, and Positano, enjoying the refreshing sea breeze and the gentle rocking of the waves.
- Sip limoncello on deck, watch colorful fishing boats bobbing on the horizon, and feel the thrill of arriving at a new port like a modern explorer.
- Prices vary depending on route and ferry company, but generally more expensive than buses.

Private Transfers: Luxury at Your Fingertips
- Indulge in comfort and convenience with a private transfer, whisking you directly to your doorstep in style.
- No need to navigate schedules or crowds, just sit back, relax, and absorb the stunning

scenery as your personal driver takes you on a scenic coastal journey.

- Ideal for larger groups, families with luggage, or those seeking a touch of luxury and VIP treatment.
- Expect higher prices compared to public transportation, but the personalized service and stress-free experience might be worth the splurge.

Taxis: Speedy Shortcuts Between Villages

- Hail a taxi for a quick and convenient way to reach neighboring villages or hidden coves not accessible by bus.
- Negotiate fares beforehand and enjoy the flexibility of hopping off at any point along the route.
- Be aware that taxi fares can be pricey, especially during peak season and late at night.
- A good option for shorter distances or when time is of the essence.

Walking: Uncovering Hidden Gems at Your Own Pace

- Lace up your shoes and embark on the Path of the Gods, a breathtaking cliffside trail connecting Positano and Nocelle, offering postcard-perfect panoramas at every turn.

- Wander through charming alleyways of colorful villages, discovering hidden piazzas, quaint shops, and secret trattorias.

- Embrace the slow pace, immerse yourself in the local atmosphere, and let your senses guide you to unexpected treasures.

- Remember, some paths can be steep and require good physical condition, so plan accordingly.

Choosing Your Chariot: Tailoring Your Amalfi Adventure

- Budget travelers and nature enthusiasts will relish the affordability and scenic vistas of buses and ferries.

- Luxury seekers and time-pressed adventurers might find private transfers ideal.
- Taxis offer convenience for short distances, while walking unlocks hidden gems and a deeper connection to the local vibe.

Day trips and transportation to nearby areas

The Amalfi Coast is a stunning destination, but there's so much more to explore in the surrounding regions. Here are some ideas for day trips and how to get there

Pompeii and Mount Vesuvius: Step back in time and explore the ancient Roman city of Pompeii, frozen in time by the eruption of Mount Vesuvius in 79 AD. Hike to the crater of the volcano for breathtaking views of the Bay of Naples.

Getting there: Take a Circumvesuviana train from Sorrento to Pompeii (about 30 minutes), then a bus or taxi to Mount Vesuvius (about 30 minutes). You can also join a guided tour from Sorrento or Naples.

Capri: This glamorous island is known for its dramatic cliffs, chic boutiques, and the Blue Grotto, a sea cave with an ethereal blue light.

Getting there: Take a ferry from Positano or Amalfi to Capri (about 40 minutes). You can also join a boat tour from Sorrento or Naples.

Naples: Italy's third-largest city offers a wealth of history, culture, and delicious food. Explore the historic center, visit the archaeological museum, or take a walk along the waterfront.

Getting there: Take a train from Sorrento to Naples (about 1 hour). You can also join a guided tour from Sorrento or Amalfi.

Paestum: This ancient Greek city is home to some of the best-preserved temples in Italy. Wander through the ruins, learn about the Greek colonists who founded the city, and enjoy the peaceful atmosphere.

Getting there: Take a train from Salerno to Paestum (about 1 hour). You can also join a guided tour from Sorrento or Amalfi.

Sorrento: This charming town is a popular base for exploring the Amalfi Coast. Wander through the narrow streets, shop for souvenirs, and enjoy the views of the sea.

Getting there: Sorrento is easily accessible by bus, train, or ferry from other towns along the Amalfi Coast.

Transportation tips

Consider purchasing a Campania Artecard: This pass gives you free or discounted entry to many museums and archaeological sites, as well as unlimited travel on public transportation in the Campania region.

Pre-book your tickets: Popular attractions like Pompeii and the Blue Grotto can get crowded, so it's a good idea to book your tickets in advance.

Be prepared for crowds: The Amalfi Coast is a popular tourist destination, so be prepared for crowds, especially in peak season.

Relax and enjoy the journey: The best way to experience the Amalfi Coast is to relax and enjoy the scenery. Take your time, explore at your own pace, and savor the Italian way of life.

Cultural Do's & Don'ts

before you dive headfirst into la dolce vita, let's equip you with the cultural compass of "do's & don'ts" to navigate this charmingly unique corner of Italy like a seasoned local.

Respecting Traditions, Embracing Warmth

Dress modestly: When visiting churches and religious sites, cover your shoulders and knees. It's a sign of respect and avoids unwanted attention.

Learn a few Italian phrases: "Buongiorno," "Grazie," and "Prego" go a long way in showing courtesy and earning smiles. Simple gestures like attempting pronunciation add to the charm.

Mind the siesta: Many shops and restaurants close for a midday break (usually 1-4 pm). Embrace the slow pace, grab a gelato, and explore quieter streets.

Tipping: It's not expected, but a small gesture (€1-2) for exceptional service is appreciated.

Queue respectfully: Patience is key in busy piazzas and shops. Avoid pushing or cutting in line, and you'll be rewarded with friendly smiles and helpfulness.

Dining Delights & Local Etiquette

Reservations recommended: Popular restaurants, especially during peak season, often require reservations. Avoid disappointment and plan ahead.

Embrace the courses: Italian meals are an experience, with antipasti, primi, secondi, and dolce in succession. Savor each course and enjoy the leisurely pace.

Leave space for limoncello: This Amalfi Coast liquid sunshine is a delightful digestif, but a small sip goes a long way!

Bread isn't for dipping: Resist the urge to dunk your bread in your soup or sauce. It's considered bad manners and might raise eyebrows.

Street food with gusto: Don't shy away from delicious street food like pizza al taglio or panino con la porchetta. It's a local favorite and a satisfying on-the-go treat.

Exploring with Awareness

Public transportation etiquette: Give up your seat for the elderly, pregnant women, and children. Stand on the right side of escalators and let people disembark before boarding.

Keep noise levels down: Be mindful of noise in quiet streets and piazzas, especially late at night. Respect the locals' desire for peaceful evenings.

Littering is a no-no: Keep the Amalfi Coast pristine by using bins and disposing of your waste responsibly. Respect the beauty of this natural paradise.

Bargaining with grace: In some shops, particularly souvenir stalls, gentle bargaining is acceptable. Do it playfully and avoid being aggressive.

Embrace the siesta atmosphere: Many towns slow down during the afternoon break. Enjoy the quiet charm, explore side streets, and appreciate the local rhythm of life.

Remember, navigating cultural nuances is part of the travel adventure. By respecting local customs and embracing the unique atmosphere, you'll earn the warm smiles and genuine hospitality that make the Amalfi Coast so special. So, dear traveler, with these "do's & don'ts" as your guide, set sail on your Amalfi adventure with confidence.

Staying Safe & Healthy

before you dive headfirst into paradise, let's make sure your Italian adventure is smooth sailing from a health and safety perspective. This chapter is your personal shield, offering practical tips and reminders to ensure your Amalfi Coast journey is as carefree as a summer breeze.

Sun Smart, Sun Strong

Sunscreen is your armor: Pack SPF 30 or higher sunscreen and reapply religiously every two hours, especially after swimming or sweating. The Mediterranean sun can be deceptive!

Seek shade at peak hours: Between 11 am and 3 pm, the sun's rays are strongest. Find refuge under umbrellas, shady cafes, or explore charming alleyways during this time.

Hydration is your ally: Carry a reusable water bottle and quench your thirst regularly. The salty air and summer heat can lead to dehydration, so stay ahead of the curve.

Headwear and sunglasses are essential: Protect your eyes and head from the sun's glare with a wide-brimmed hat and UV-protective sunglasses.

Navigating the Terrain with Confidence
Shoes for every adventure: Pack sturdy walking shoes for exploring cliffside paths and charming villages. Avoid slippery flip-flops, especially on uneven terrain.

Be mindful of water currents: Don't overestimate your swimming abilities. Stick to patrolled beaches and follow red flag warnings during rough seas.

Respect private property: Many coastal areas are private beaches or rocky cliffs. Stay within designated swimming areas and avoid trespassing on private property.

Practice common sense: Don't climb dangerous cliffs, swim while intoxicated, or leave valuables unattended on the beach. A little caution goes a long way.

Staying Healthy and Happy

Travel insurance is your safety net: Invest in travel insurance to cover unexpected medical expenses or trip cancellations. It's always better to be safe than sorry.

Pack essential medications: Bring any medications you regularly use, along with over-the-counter remedies for common ailments like headaches or upset stomachs.

Stay informed about local health updates: Check with your local embassy or consulate about any health advisories for the Amalfi Coast before your trip.

Be mindful of food hygiene: Stick to reputable restaurants and cafes, avoid undercooked seafood, and drink bottled water when in doubt.

Wash your hands regularly: Keep hand sanitizer handy and wash your hands frequently, especially before meals and after using public restrooms.

Remember, prioritizing your health and safety doesn't diminish the adventure, it enhances it! By taking these simple precautions, you can fully embrace the magic of the Amalfi Coast with peace of mind, knowing you've laid the foundation for a healthy and joyful experience.

CHAPTER 3

Where to Stay

This chapter is your key to unlocking diverse havens, from cliffside castles to cozy B&Bs and seaside chic hotels, ensuring your stay reflects your unique travel dreams.

Positano's Cascading Charm

Cliffside luxury: Perched like colorful jewels on dramatic cliffs, Positano's luxury hotels offer breathtaking panoramas, infinity pools, and pampering spa treatments. Think private infinity pools overlooking the turquoise sea and romantic terraces bathed in sunset hues.

Boutique bliss: Nestled in narrow lanes, charming boutique hotels with vibrantly tiled floors and lemon tree courtyards ooze local character. Savor fresh pastries on quaint balconies and immerse yourself in the village's vibrant energy.

Amalfi's Historical Elegance

Grand hotels: Steeped in history, Amalfi's grand hotels boast frescoed ceilings, marble floors, and seafront terraces overlooking the bustling harbor. Imagine indulging in afternoon tea with sea views and exploring ancient alleyways just steps away.

Family-friendly havens: Warmly welcoming families, Amalfi offers spacious apartments and guesthouses with private kitchens and close proximity to beaches. Picture sandy-toed fun on the shore followed by cozy evenings on balconies overlooking the twinkling town.

Ravello's Hilltop Enchantment

Luxury villas: Escape to hillside havens amidst lush gardens, infinity pools overlooking valleys, and private terraces draped in bougainvillea. Think private chefs preparing alfresco dinners and panoramic views that steal your breath away.

Romantic hideaways: Tucked away amidst lemon groves, boutique hotels with intimate terraces and cozy fireplaces offer a haven for romance. Picture candlelit dinners on secluded balconies and watching the sun paint the sky with golden hues.

Budget-Conscious Gems

B&Bs and guesthouses: For a taste of local life and budget-friendly charm, B&Bs and guesthouses in smaller villages offer cozy rooms, friendly hosts, and delicious homemade breakfasts. Imagine sharing stories with fellow travelers over steaming cups of cappuccino and exploring hidden coves nearby.

Agritourism retreats: Immerse yourself in the heart of Amalfi's countryside with agritourism stays. Imagine waking up to the scent of fresh bread and exploring rolling hills dotted with olive groves and vineyards, all while enjoying comfortable accommodations and authentic meals.

.

Hotels, resorts, and bed-and-breakfast options

The Amalfi Coast, with its vibrant towns, dramatic cliffs, and turquoise waters, beckons travelers with its unique charm. But choosing the right accommodation can feel overwhelming with the variety of hotels, resorts, and bed-and-breakfasts available. Fear not, discerning traveler! This guide will help you navigate the options, ensuring your stay perfectly reflects your budget, preferences, and desired Amalfi Coast experience.

Luxury Indulgence: Hotels and Resorts
- Grand Hotel Excelsior Vittoria (Sorrento): This iconic hotel offers unparalleled luxury, breathtaking sea views, Michelin-starred dining, and impeccable service. Perfect for those seeking ultimate pampering and a touch of history.

- Monastero Santa Rosa Hotel & Spa (Conca dei Marini): Housed in a converted 17th-century monastery, this luxurious resort boasts cliffside infinity pools, a spa with breathtaking views, and elegant rooms with private balconies.

- **Santa Caterina (Amalfi):** This historic hotel offers a blend of traditional charm and modern amenities, with stunning sea views, a private beach club, and a Michelin-starred restaurant.

Boutique Charm: Hotels and B&Bs

- **La Minerva (Ravello):** This charming hotel features individually decorated rooms, a rooftop terrace with panoramic views, and a peaceful location close to the Duomo.

- **Palazzo Murat (Positano):** Housed in a historic 18th-century palace, this boutique hotel offers personalized service, comfortable rooms with balconies, and stunning views of Positano's colorful houses.

- **Villa Tre Ville (Praiano):** This family-run B&B offers a warm and welcoming atmosphere, spacious rooms with balconies, and a delicious breakfast overlooking the sea.

Authentic Experiences: B&Bs and Agriturismos

- **Residenza Il Cavatappi (Amalfi):** This charming B&B housed in a traditional building offers a local experience with cozy rooms, personalized service, and a rooftop terrace with stunning views.

- **Locanda Lorelei (Ravello):** Immerse yourself in the local culture at this family-run B&B, known for its delicious home-cooked meals, friendly atmosphere, and panoramic sea views.

- **Agriturismo Il Raddo (Tramonti):** Experience the beauty of the Amalfi countryside at this working farm, offering comfortable rooms, delicious farm-to-table meals, and breathtaking mountain views.

Beyond the Obvious

- **Consider your budget:** Luxury hotels and resorts offer unparalleled experiences, but come at a premium price. B&Bs and agriturismos provide a more budget-friendly option with a local touch.

- **Location matters:** Do you crave the heart of the action or peaceful seclusion? Choose a town that aligns with your desired atmosphere.

- **Amenities are key:** Prioritize features like sea views, swimming pools, balconies, or proximity to specific sights.

- **Read reviews:** Gain valuable insights from previous guests about the atmosphere, amenities, and overall experience offered by different accommodations.

- **Embrace local experiences:** Many B&Bs and agriturismos offer cooking classes, wine tastings, or excursions, allowing you to delve deeper into the local culture.

Remember, your Amalfi Coast haven is more than just a place to sleep. It's your base for exploring, relaxing, and creating unforgettable memories. Choose wisely, based on your priorities, and let your accommodation enhance your journey!

Additional Resources

- Booking.com
- Airbnb
- TripAdvisor
- Amalfi Coast official website

Location-based recommendations

Remember, choosing your accommodation goes beyond just finding a place to sleep, it's about setting the foundation for your entire Amalfi Coast experience. To help you find the perfect fit, consider these location-specific recommendations:

Town-by-Town Guide

Positano: Crave the iconic cliffside views and vibrant atmosphere? Opt for centrally located hotels with balconies or terraces, or charming B&Bs tucked away in narrow streets.

Amalfi: Seek historical charm and convenient access to town attractions? Choose hotels near the Duomo or harbor, or B&Bs in traditional buildings for a local touch.

Ravello: Yearn for peaceful seclusion and breathtaking panoramas? Boutique hotels with infinity pools and sea views or family-run B&Bs nestled in the hills offer tranquility.

Praiano: Desire a budget-friendly option with a local feel? Consider family-run guesthouses or agriturismos in the countryside, offering home-cooked meals and stunning mountain views.

Sorrento: Seeking a lively town with excellent transportation links? Choose hotels near the main square or harbor, or opt for B&Bs in quieter residential areas.

Beyond Town Centers

Secluded Beachfront: For ultimate privacy and direct access to the sea, consider luxury resorts or vacation rentals in hidden coves like Conca dei Marini or Marina del Cantone.

Hillside Serenity: Immerse yourself in the rural charm of the Amalfi Coast hinterland with agriturismos offering farm stays, breathtaking mountain views, and authentic dining experiences.

Unique Stays: Experience a touch of history by staying in converted monasteries like Monastero Santa Rosa, or indulge in luxury cliffside villas with private pools and unparalleled panoramas.

Personalize Your Search

Remember, these are just starting points. Use online platforms and this guidebook to filter your search based on specific amenities, budgets, and desired experiences. Look for reviews to gain insights into the atmosphere and service offered by different accommodations.

By considering your location preferences and desired experience, you can find the perfect Amalfi Coast haven that complements your dream vacation!

CHAPTER 4

Destinations

The Amalfi Coast, with its dramatic cliffs cascading into turquoise waters and charming towns clinging to hillsides, offers an abundance of destinations for discerning travelers. Beyond the postcard-perfect views, each village boasts unique personalities, historical riches, and cultural experiences waiting to be discovered. So, lace up your walking shoes, pack your sense of adventure, and let's embark on a journey through some of the most captivating destinations along this enchanting coastline:

Positano

- Unveiling the Picture-Perfect Paradise: Positano's iconic image, with pastel-colored houses cascading down cliffs towards the sea, needs no introduction. Wander through narrow streets lined with boutiques, savor fresh seafood on a terrace overlooking the beach, and soak up the vibrant atmosphere.

- Beyond the Beauty: Explore the Church of Santa Maria Assunta with its captivating black Madonna, embark on a boat trip to hidden coves and grottos, or hike the Path of the Gods for breathtaking panoramas.

Amalfi

- Tracing Centuries of Splendor: Immerse yourself in the town's rich history as a former maritime republic. Discover the majestic Duomo adorned with mosaics, marvel at the Chiostro del Paradiso's tranquil cloister, and explore the Paper Museum, a testament to Amalfi's unique craft.

- A Foodie's Delight: Savor fresh seafood dishes, indulge in homemade pasta creations, and don't miss the chance to try the iconic limoncello liqueur, born and perfected in Amalfi.

Ravello

- Where Luxury Meets Tranquility: Nestled atop the cliffs, Ravello offers a haven of peace and breathtaking vistas. Wander through its elegant gardens, marvel at the architectural beauty of Villa Rufolo and Villa Cimbrone, and enjoy the world-renowned Ravello Music Festival during the summer months.

- **Beyond the Gardens:** Explore the quaint Piazza del Duomo, discover the history of the Coral Museum, and embark on a scenic walk along the Valle delle Ferriere, a lush gorge with cascading waterfalls.

Praiano

- **A Breath of Fresh Air:** Escape the bustling crowds and discover the authentic charm of Praiano. Wander through its quiet streets adorned with bougainvillea, relax on its secluded beaches, and enjoy the stunning views of the coastline from its many viewpoints.

- **Off the Beaten Path:** Explore the Church of San Gennaro with its captivating frescoes, embark on a boat tour to discover hidden grottos, and savor delicious local cuisine at family-run restaurants.

Sorrento

- Lively Charm and Cultural Crossroads: Sorrento offers a vibrant mix of history, culture, and modern amenities. Explore the historic center, visit the Museo Correale showcasing Roman artifacts, and wander through the bustling Piazza Tasso, known for its cafes and shops.

- Beyond the Main Square: Take a scenic walk along the Marina Grande, explore the lemon orchards and olive groves surrounding the town, and join a cooking class to learn the secrets of authentic Sorrentine cuisine.

Hidden Gems

- Atrani: A tiny fisherman's village offering a glimpse into traditional Amalfi life, featuring colorful houses, a charming beach, and the Church of Santa Maria Maddalena with its majolica tile floor.

- **Vietri sul Mare:** Renowned for its colorful ceramics, this town offers a vibrant artistic scene, charming workshops, and breathtaking views of the coastline.

- **Conca dei Marini:** Immerse yourself in the legend of Emerald Grotto, accessible only by boat, and explore the historic watchtowers guarding the coastline.

Remember, This is just a starting point. Each town offers unique experiences and hidden treasures waiting to be discovered. Explore at your own pace, embrace the local atmosphere, and create memories that will last a lifetime!

Additional Tips

- Consider purchasing a Campania Artecard for discounted entry to museums and archaeological sites, and unlimited travel on public transportation.
- Download offline maps and bus schedules to navigate with ease, especially in smaller towns.
- Be prepared for crowds, especially during peak season.
- Embrace the Italian laid-back attitude, patience and a smile go a long way!

Historical background

Amalfi, nestled along the breathtaking Amalfi Coast, isn't just a place of captivating beauty, it's a living testament to a rich and vibrant history. As you wander its charming streets, imagine bustling merchants, powerful maritime republics, and the echoes of centuries whispering forgotten tales. Let's embark on a journey through time and delve into Amalfi's captivating past:

From Humble Beginnings to Maritime Might

- A.D. 839: Our story begins with the foundation of the Republic of Amalfi, marking the dawn of an era of power and prosperity. Imagine its rise from a small maritime community to a dominant force in the Mediterranean, controlling trade routes and forging alliances.

- Rivals and Riches: Witness Amalfi's fierce competition with neighboring Pisa and Venice, vying for control of the lucrative spice trade. Picture ships laden with treasures arriving at the bustling harbor, enriching the town and fueling its architectural marvels.

- A Legacy in Stone: Marvel at the Duomo, a UNESCO World Heritage Site, its intricate mosaics and architecture reflecting the wealth and artistry of the republic's golden age. Imagine the Duomo's construction, a collaborative effort by skilled artisans and a symbol of Amalfi's pride.

The Paper Trail: A Unique Craft Endures

- A.D. 13th Century: Discover the unique tradition of Amalfi paper, prized for its strength, beauty, and durability. Used for centuries for important documents, even royal correspondence, imagine scribes carefully crafting these sheets, their delicate script whispering secrets of the past.

- Unveiling the Papermaking Process: Step into the Paper Museum, a window into this fascinating craft. Learn about the intricate hand-beating methods, the use of local water sources, and the enduring legacy of Amalfi's papermakers.

- **A Treasured Souvenir:** As you admire the delicate paper creations, consider taking home a unique piece, a tangible reminder of this centuries-old tradition.

From Republic to Modern Marvel

- **1806:** Witness the decline of the Republic due to various factors, including shifting trade routes and political turmoil. Imagine the once-powerful republic adapting to changing times, transitioning into a charming town cherished for its beauty and cultural heritage.

- **A Destination Emerges:** Fast forward to the 19th century and picture Amalfi reborn as a captivating tourist destination. Imagine artists and writers drawn to its picturesque landscapes, and travelers seeking its sun-kissed shores and historical allure.

- **Preserving the Past:** Today, Amalfi strives to balance its historical character with modern life. Observe restoration efforts, cultural events celebrating its heritage, and a community dedicated to preserving its unique story.

Remember, Amalfi's history isn't just dates and facts, it's woven into the very fabric of the town. As you explore, imagine the echoes of the past, the lives lived, and the stories waiting to be unearthed. Embrace the historical richness that adds depth and wonder to your Amalfi experience.

Additional Tips
- Visit the Civic Museum for a more comprehensive overview of Amalfi's history, showcasing artifacts and exhibits spanning different eras.
- Engage with local artisans and shopkeepers, many of whom carry family traditions and historical knowledge passed down through generations.

- Consider joining a guided historical walking tour to gain deeper insights and hidden stories of the town's past.

Amalfi & Top attractions

Whether you're a history buff, a foodie, or simply seeking a slice of Italian enchantment, Amalfi offers something for every wanderer. So, unpack your curiosity, lace up your walking shoes, and let's delve into this captivating town:

Step Back in Time

-Witness Maritime Grandeur: The majestic Duomo, a UNESCO World Heritage Site, stands as a testament to Amalfi's glorious past as a powerful maritime republic. Marvel at its awe-inspiring mosaics, intricate architecture, and imagine merchants bustling about and ships laden with treasures arriving in the harbor.

- Unravel Paper-Making Secrets: Discover the unique tradition of Amalfi paper, used for centuries for important documents and even royal correspondence. Step inside the Paper Museum, learn about its delicate creation process, and be mesmerized by its beauty.

- **Wander Through Centuries:** Lose yourself in the labyrinthine streets of the historic center, lined with medieval buildings, piazzas adorned with fountains, and hidden archways whispering tales of the past. Breathe in the atmosphere and feel the town's rich history come alive.

Indulge Your Senses
- **Seafood Symphony:** From succulent grilled octopus to flavorful spaghetti alle vongole (clams), Amalfi's restaurants showcase the freshest seafood, boasting the bounty of the nearby waters. Savor the taste of the sea with every bite.

- **Limoncello Bliss:** Discover the birthplace of the iconic limoncello liqueur, a refreshing and zesty delight infused with the sunshine-kissed Amalfi lemons. Visit local producers, witness the traditional process, and indulge in a taste of sunshine.

- **Shopping Delights:** Browse through charming boutiques brimming with colorful ceramics, hand-crafted leather goods, and locally woven textiles. Find unique souvenirs that capture the essence of Amalfi's artistry and craftsmanship.

Uncover Hidden Gems
- Seek Tranquility at the Chiostro del Paradiso: Tucked away within the Duomo complex lies this oasis of serenity. Admire the peaceful cloister adorned with intricate marble columns and lush greenery, offering a welcome respite from the bustling town center.

- Discover Artistic Beauty: Unearth the Fontana Sant'Andrea, a hidden gem adorned with stunning majolica tiles depicting scenes from the life of Saint Andrew, Amalfi's patron saint. Let the artistry and history transport you.

- Embrace Nature's Beauty: Embark on a scenic walk through the lush Valle delle Ferriere, following the ancient path used to transport papermaking materials. Witness cascading waterfalls, encounter remnants of old mills, and immerse yourself in Amalfi's natural splendor.

Unforgettable Experiences

Boat Tour: Embark on a scenic boat tour along the Amalfi Coast, marveling at the dramatic cliffs plunging into the turquoise waters, exploring hidden coves, and soaking in the breathtaking panoramas from a unique perspective. Capture postcard-perfect moments and feel the refreshing sea breeze as you cruise along the coastline.

Cooking Class: Immerse yourself in the local culinary traditions by joining a cooking class. Learn the secrets of preparing authentic Amalfi dishes, using fresh seasonal ingredients and traditional techniques. Enjoy the fruits of your labor with a delicious meal you created yourself, savoring the flavors and memories.

Hiking: Lace up your walking shoes and explore the Amalfi Coast on foot. Hike along scenic trails overlooking the sea, breathe in the fresh air, and discover hidden gems like secluded beaches and quaint villages. Challenge yourself with breathtaking climbs and reward yourself with panoramic vistas.

Remember, Amalfi is more than just a destination it's an experience. Soak in the vibrant atmosphere, engage with the friendly locals, and savor the unique blend of history, culture, and delectable cuisine. Let Amalfi weave its magic around you, creating memories that will forever linger in your heart.

Additional Tips

- Consider joining a guided walking tour to gain deeper insights into Amalfi's history and hidden gems.
- Be prepared for some uphill walking, especially in the historic center. Wear comfortable shoes and embrace the scenic climbs.

- Combine your visit to Amalfi with exploring nearby towns like Ravello or Atrani for a diverse Amalfi Coast experience.

Exploring Atrani: A Hidden Gem

Step away from the bustling crowds and vibrant energy of Amalfi, and step into Atrani, a hidden gem nestled between dramatic cliffs, where time seems to slow down and tranquility reigns supreme. This charming village, often overshadowed by its larger neighbor, offers a unique experience for travelers seeking an authentic Italian escape.

A Picture-Perfect Postcard

Quaint Charm: Imagine strolling through narrow, flower-adorned lanes, past pastel-colored houses with terracotta roofs. The main square, Piazza Umberto I, pulsates with the gentle murmur of conversations and the aroma of freshly baked bread wafting from the local panetteria.

Beach Bliss: Bask on the shingle beach, lapped by crystal-clear turquoise waters. Soak up the sun, dip into the refreshing sea, or simply relax with a good book under the Mediterranean sun. Atrani's beach, though small, offers a serene escape from the crowds.

Architectural Gems: Discover the 12th-century Santa Maria Maddalena Cathedral, a stunning example of Romanesque architecture. Admire the intricate details of the facade, step inside to be awestruck by the colorful mosaics, and savor the tranquility within its ancient walls.

Beyond the Usual

Cliffside Climb: Hike up the winding path to the Church of San Salvatore de Birecto, perched atop a cliff overlooking the village. The breathtaking panoramic views encompass the Amalfi Coast in all its glory, offering a sense of peaceful isolation and a reward for your effort.

Lemon Groves & Local Flavors: Immerse yourself in the agritourism experience at a local farm nestled amidst lemon groves. Learn about the traditional production methods, savor farm-to-table meals bursting with fresh, seasonal flavors, and perhaps even participate in a cooking class to unlock the secrets of Amalfi cuisine.

Hidden Waterfalls: Hike along the Valle delle Ferriere, a lush green valley leading to hidden waterfalls cascading into natural pools. Take a refreshing dip, explore the scenic trails, and enjoy the serenity of this secluded haven.

Experiences for the Soul

Art & Crafts: Discover the creative spirit of Atrani by browsing local artisan shops. Find unique hand-painted ceramics, intricate lacework, and locally crafted jewelry, each piece imbued with the character and traditions of the village.

Live Music & Local Events: Immerse yourself in the heart of Atrani's culture by attending a live music performance in the piazza, often featuring traditional Neapolitan songs and lively melodies. Participate in local festivals, like the Festa di San

Michele in September, and experience the warmth and joy of the community spirit.

Stargazing under the Mediterranean Sky: Escape the light pollution and witness the Milky Way in all its glory on a clear night. Find a quiet spot on the beach or atop the cliffs, and be mesmerized by the vastness of the universe twinkling above the tranquil village.

Remember

- Atrani is a pedestrian-only village, so comfortable shoes are essential.
- Pack light clothes and swimwear for enjoying the beach and exploring the surrounding area.
- Embrace the slow pace of life and savor the simple pleasures of this charming village.
- Respect the local culture and traditions by being mindful of noise levels and dressing modestly when visiting religious sites.

Local cuisine and dining recommendations

Amalfi's charm extends far beyond its captivating landscapes and historical treasures. The town boasts a vibrant culinary scene, where fresh, local ingredients are transformed into delectable dishes that tantalize the taste buds and embody the spirit of the Amalfi Coast. So, embark on a delicious adventure with these local cuisine recommendations and hidden dining gems.

Embracing Sea-to-Plate Delights

Fresh Seafood Feasts: Indulge in the bounty of the Tyrrhenian Sea with an authentic "frutti di mare" experience. Savor succulent grilled octopus, flavorful spaghetti alle vongole (clams), or a steaming bowl of zuppa di pesce (fish soup), each dish bursting with freshness and showcasing the expertise of local fishermen.

Pasta Perfection: From the iconic spaghetti alle vongole to the local favorite, scialatielli with seafood sauce, Amalfi's pasta dishes are an art form. Don't miss the chance to try handmade gnocchi with pesto or indulge in the simplicity of a perfectly cooked pomodoro (tomato) sauce pasta.

Lemons in Every Bite: The ubiquitous Amalfi lemon adds a zesty twist to various dishes. Sample flavorful grilled fish drizzled with lemon sauce, savor a refreshing caprese salad adorned with lemon zest, or indulge in a light and fluffy lemon cake for dessert.

Hidden Gems for Discerning Foodies
Ristorante La Caravella: Perched on a cliff overlooking the sea, this renowned restaurant offers spectacular views and an upscale dining experience. Enjoy fresh seafood specialties and traditional Amalfi dishes in an elegant ambiance.

La Cucina di Mamma: Experience the warmth and authenticity of home-cooked Amalfi cuisine at this family-run trattoria. Savor fresh pastas, local ingredients prepared with love, and a cozy atmosphere for an unforgettable dining experience.

Pasticceria Andrea Pansa: Indulge your sweet tooth at this historic pasticceria, famed for its delectable pastries and traditional limoncello. Sample sfogliatelle, cannoli, and other sweet treats, handcrafted with generations-old recipes.

Local Delights Beyond Restaurants

Mercato del Pesce: Witness the vibrant energy of the local fish market, bustling with fishermen selling their fresh catch. Immerse yourself in the sights and smells, perhaps selecting ingredients for your own Amalfi-inspired meal.

Limoncello Producers: Visit a local limoncello producer, learn about the traditional production process, and savor the iconic liqueur straight from the source. Many offer tastings and insights into this Amalfi staple.

Paniini Perfection: Grab a freshly made panini from a local shop, filled with local cheeses, cured meats, and fresh vegetables. It's a delicious and convenient option for a quick lunch or picnic with a view.

Atrani

Simple yet Spectacular: Atrani's culinary scene focuses on fresh, seasonal ingredients and traditional dishes prepared with care. Savor homemade ravioli with local ricotta and herbs at L'Arco, or enjoy a plate of spaghetti al pomodoro with the freshest tomatoes at La Sportella.

Pizza Perfection: Don't miss the chance to try pizza made the Amalfi way, with thin crusts and simple toppings showcasing the quality of local ingredients. L'Incanto and La Tortuga offer delicious wood-fired pizzas perfect for a casual lunch or dinner.

Hidden Gems: Venture beyond the main square and discover hidden culinary gems like La Giara or Locanda Severino. These intimate trattorias offer unique twists on local dishes, using seasonal ingredients and creative presentations to delight your senses.

Remember: When dining in Amalfi, embrace the slow-paced lifestyle. Savor the flavors, connect with the friendly locals, and enjoy the unique atmosphere. Don't forget to pair your meal with a glass of locally produced wine for an authentic culinary experience. Most restaurants close for lunch between 3-5 pm and reopen for dinner around 8 pm. Many establishments accept cash only, so be prepared. Don't be afraid to try new things and ask for recommendations! Locals are passionate about their food and love to share their favorites.

Additional Tips

- Consider joining a food tour to discover hidden gems, learn about local food traditions, and sample various specialties.
- Make reservations in advance, especially for popular restaurants during peak season.
- Be prepared for some restaurants to have limited English menus, but embrace the opportunity to explore and experiment with new flavors.
- Enjoy the "al fresco" dining experience and soak up the Amalfi atmosphere while savoring your meal.

Discover the unique wines of the Amalfi Coast, characterized by their minerality and citrusy notes. Visit a local winery like Marisa Cuomo or Cantina Amalfi for a guided tasting and learn about the region's viticulture traditions.

CHAPTER 5

Positano

The crown jewel of the Amalfi Coast! Prepare to be mesmerized by its iconic pastel-colored houses cascading down dramatic cliffs, turquoise waters lapping at charming beaches, and an atmosphere imbued with romance, charm, and breathtaking beauty. This chapter will be your guide to navigating Positano like a pro, ensuring your stay is filled with unforgettable experiences.

Sun-Kissed Shores and Hidden Coves

- Fornillo & Marina Grande: Immerse yourself in the classic Positano beach experience. Relax on sun loungers at Fornillo, a pebble beach accessible by footpath or boat, or enjoy the larger Marina Grande with its vibrant atmosphere and water sports options.

- Spiaggia Laurito & Fiumariello: Seek hidden gems further down the coast. Hike along the Path of

the Gods for breathtaking views and reach the
secluded Spiaggia Laurito, or discover the charming
cove of Fiumariello accessible only by boat.

Beyond the Beaches
- **Wander the Labyrinthine Streets:** Get lost in the
maze of narrow alleyways lined with colorful
houses, charming boutiques showcasing local crafts,
and art galleries bursting with creativity. Savor the
slow pace, embrace the vibrant atmosphere, and get
swept away by Positano's unique charm.

- **Church of Santa Maria Assunta:** Witness the
iconic landmark dominating the Positano skyline.
Admire the majolica tile dome, explore the intricate
interior, and marvel at the Black Madonna, patron
saint of Positano.

- **Path of the Gods:** Embark on an unforgettable
hike along this legendary trail, offering panoramic
views of the coastline, hidden coves, and dramatic
cliffs. Breathe in the fresh air, capture breathtaking

photos, and experience the natural beauty surrounding Positano.

Culinary Delights

- **Fresh Seafood Feasts**: Savor the bounty of the sea at waterfront restaurants or hidden trattorias. Indulge in spaghetti alle vongole (clams), grilled octopus, or local fish specialties, each dish bursting with freshness and capturing the essence of Positano's culinary heritage.

- **Lemons in Every Bite:** The ubiquitous Amalfi lemon adds a zesty twist to Positano's cuisine. Sample flavorful pasta dishes with lemon sauce, indulge in a refreshing caprese salad, or savor a light and fluffy lemon cake for dessert.

- **Sunset Aperitivo Ritual:** Experience the quintessential Positano ritual. Sip on a refreshing drink, nibble on local delicacies, and soak up the breathtaking sunset views from a panoramic terrace, creating memories that will last a lifetime.

Accommodation Choices

- **Luxury Cliffside Hotels:** Immerse yourself in ultimate luxury with breathtaking sea views and impeccable service. Opt for private balconies, infinity pools, and stunning interiors for an unforgettable Positano experience.

- **Charming Boutique Hotels:** Find your haven in intimate boutique hotels nestled within the historical center. Enjoy personalized service, local charm, and easy access to Positano's vibrant heart.

- **Budget-Friendly Options:** Discover comfortable guesthouses or family-run B&Bs nestled in quieter corners. Enjoy a more local experience, friendly interactions, and budget-conscious options without compromising on the Positano charm.

Tips & Tricks

- Wear comfortable shoes for exploring the hilly streets and navigating stairs.

- Consider purchasing a Campania Artecard for discounted entry to museums and public transportation.
- Be prepared for crowds, especially during peak season. Book accommodations and reservations in advance.
- Embrace the Italian laid-back attitude, patience and a smile go a long way!

Remember, Positano is more than just a destination, it's an experience. Embrace the dolce vita lifestyle, connect with the friendly locals, and create memories that will forever paint your heart with the vibrant colors of this enchanting cliffside paradise.

Exploring Praiano: A Serene Getaway

Step away from the bustling crowds and picture-perfect chaos of Positano, and discover Praiano, a hidden gem nestled along the Amalfi Coast. This charming village offers a serene escape, where time slows down, and the breathtaking beauty of the Mediterranean unfolds before you.

A Tranquil Haven

Quaint Charm: Wander through narrow, flower-adorned lanes lined with pastel-colored houses bathed in warm sunlight. Explore hidden piazzas where the gentle murmur of conversations mingles with the scent of freshly baked bread, and feel the tranquility seep into your soul.

Marina di Praia: Bask on the shingle beach lapped by crystal-clear turquoise waters. Soak up the sun, cool off with a refreshing dip, or explore the rocky coves offering a sense of privacy and hidden beauty.

Church of San Gennaro: This 12th-century church perched on a hilltop offers not just spiritual solace but also panoramic views that encompass the vastness of the coastline and the charming village below.

Torre a Mare: Hike up to this ancient watchtower, a silent sentinel guarding the coastline for centuries. Enjoy the breathtaking vistas, imagine the stories whispered by the wind, and feel a sense of timeless serenity.

Beyond the Usual

Hidden Beaches: Discover secluded coves like Cala Gaviota and Cala Marina di Nova, accessible only by foot or boat. Find your own patch of paradise, listen to the gentle lapping of waves, and immerse yourself in the tranquility of nature.

Lemon Groves & Local Flavors: Immerse yourself in the agritourism experience at a local farm nestled amidst lemon groves. Learn about traditional production methods, savor farm-to-table meals bursting with fresh, seasonal flavors, and perhaps even participate in a cooking class to unlock the secrets of Amalfi cuisine.

Art & Crafts: Discover the creative spirit of Praiano by browsing local artisan shops. Find unique hand-painted ceramics, intricate lacework, and locally crafted jewelry, each piece imbued with the character and traditions of the village.

Stargazing Paradise: Escape the light pollution and witness the Milky Way in all its glory on a clear night. Find a quiet spot on the beach or atop a hill, and be mesmerized by the vastness of the universe twinkling above the tranquil village.

Experiences for the Soul
Boat Tours & Grotto Explorations: Embark on a boat trip along the rugged coastline, discovering hidden grottos like the Emerald Grotto, where

sunlight creates an ethereal display of colors on the water's surface.

Hiking & Nature Trails: Lace up your shoes and explore the scenic trails that weave through olive groves and vineyards, offering breathtaking views and a chance to connect with nature's serenity.

Live Music & Local Events: Immerse yourself in the heart of Praiano's culture by attending a live music performance in the piazza, often featuring traditional Neapolitan songs and lively melodies. Participate in local festivals, like the Festa di San Luca in October, and experience the warmth and joy of the community spirit.

Remember

- Praiano is a car-free village, so comfortable shoes are essential.
- Pack light clothes and swimwear for enjoying the beaches and exploring the surrounding area.

- Embrace the slow pace of life and savor the simple pleasures of this charming village.
- Respect the local culture and traditions by being mindful of noise levels and dressing modestly when visiting religious sites.

Hiking the Path of the Gods

Imagine yourself winding through ancient trails cloaked in history, breathtaking coastal views unfolding at every turn, and the refreshing Mediterranean breeze caressing your face. Welcome to the Path of the Gods (Sentiero degli Dei), a legendary hike starting in Praiano, promising an unforgettable adventure for nature lovers and history buffs alike.

Starting your Path of the Gods journey from Praiano offers unique advantages

Escape the Crowds: Unlike the usual Bomerano starting point, Praiano provides a quieter experience, allowing you to fully immerse yourself in the natural beauty and historical significance of the trail.

Hidden Gems: Embark on the Praiano Variante, an alternative route showcasing hidden beaches, charming villages like Marina di Praia, and the iconic Torre a Mare watchtower.

Gradual Ascent: Unlike the sharply inclined Bomerano section, Praiano offers a more gradual climb, perfect for hikers of all levels.

Unveiling the Path

Breathtaking Panorama: As you leave Praiano behind, the trail unfolds, revealing the vast expanse of the Amalfi Coast in all its splendor. Azure waters lap at dramatic cliffs, colorful villages cling to hillsides, and the horizon stretches towards the endless blue.

Ancient Roman Footpath: Immerse yourself in history as you walk along the same path used by Romans for centuries. Imagine legions marching, traders carrying goods, and everyday life unfolding on this historic artery.

Flora & Fauna: Breathe in the fragrant scent of Mediterranean herbs, spot lizards basking on sun-drenched rocks, and witness birds soaring high above the cliffs. The path teems with life, adding another layer to your sensory experience.

Beyond the Walk

Secluded Beaches: Reward yourself with refreshing dips in hidden coves like Cala Gaviota or Marina di Nova, accessible only by foot or boat. Bask on the pebbled shores, swim in crystal-clear waters, and soak up the tranquility amidst the dramatic cliffs.

Local Food & Culture: Stop by a family-run trattoria in Nocelle or Positano for a delicious lunch featuring fresh seafood, homemade pasta, and local wines. Savor the flavors of the Amalfi Coast while interacting with the warm and welcoming community.

Historical Gems: Explore the Church of Santa Maria Assunta in Positano, adorned with a captivating majolica dome, or discover the ancient ruins of a Roman villa in Bomerano, whispering tales of a bygone era.

Tips & Recommendations

- Start early to avoid the midday heat, especially during peak season.
- Wear comfortable hiking shoes with good grip and sun protection.
- Bring plenty of water and snacks for the journey.
- Consider a guided tour for historical insights and local anecdotes.
- Respect the environment and leave no trace on the trail.

Beaches and outdoor activities

Whether you seek relaxation on sun-drenched beaches or crave active pursuits, Positano delivers an outdoor experience unlike any other. Dive into this chapter and discover your perfect blend of coastal bliss and adventurous exploration:

Beachside Bliss

- Fornillo Beach: Immerse yourself in the classic Positano beach experience. Relax on sun loungers, rent a paddleboard to explore the turquoise waters, or savor fresh seafood at waterfront restaurants. Enjoy the vibrant atmosphere and soak up the sun.

- Marina Grande Beach: This larger beach offers a mix of relaxation and watersports. Enjoy sunbathing, swimming, or try your hand at kayaking or stand-up paddleboarding. Relax at beachside cafes and restaurants, soaking in the laid-back Mediterranean vibes.

- **Spiaggia Laurito:** Hike along the Path of the Gods for breathtaking views and reach this secluded gem. With limited accessibility and crystal-clear waters, it's perfect for escaping the crowds and experiencing unspoiled beauty.

Adventurous Pursuits

- **Path of the Gods Hike:** Embark on this legendary trail, offering panoramic views of the coastline, hidden coves, and dramatic cliffs. Breathe in the fresh air, capture stunning photos, and challenge yourself with scenic climbs.

- **Boat Tours:** Explore the Amalfi Coast from a different perspective. Discover hidden coves, secluded beaches, and charming villages accessible only by sea. Swim in grottos, snorkel in pristine waters, and capture the breathtaking beauty of the coastline.

- **Kayaking & Stand-Up Paddleboarding:** Glide along the turquoise waters at your own pace, exploring hidden coves and dramatic cliffs from a unique vantage point. Enjoy the refreshing sea breeze and feel the rhythm of the waves.

Beyond the Beaches
- **Scuba Diving & Snorkeling:** Discover the underwater world teeming with colorful marine life. Explore hidden reefs, shipwrecks, and fascinating rock formations in crystal-clear waters. Witness the vibrant biodiversity and create unforgettable memories beneath the waves.

- **Paragliding:** Soar above the Amalfi Coast, experiencing breathtaking views from a bird's-eye perspective. Witness the dramatic cliffs plunging into the sea, colorful villages clinging to the hillsides, and the endless expanse of the Mediterranean.

- **Cooking Classes:** Immerse yourself in local culinary traditions by joining a cooking class. Learn the secrets of preparing authentic Positano dishes, using fresh seasonal ingredients and traditional techniques. Enjoy the fruits of your labor with a delicious meal you created yourself.

Remember

- Wear comfortable shoes and sun protection for outdoor activities.
- Consider booking boat tours and activities in advance, especially during peak season.
- Respect the local environment and follow sustainable practices while exploring the beaches and natural areas.
- Embrace the "dolce vita" lifestyle and savor the beauty and tranquility of Positano's unique offerings.

Additional Tips

- Purchase a Campania Artecard for discounted entry to museums and public transportation.
- Be prepared for some beaches to have limited facilities, so pack accordingly.
- Learn some basic Italian phrases to enhance your interaction with locals.
- Enjoy the fresh seafood dishes and local wines for a truly authentic Positano experience.

Shopping and nightlife options

Positano isn't just a beach paradise, it's a haven for discerning shoppers and those seeking vibrant nightlife experiences. From indulging in local crafts to exploring trendy boutiques and enjoying lively bars, prepare to be surprised by the hidden gems and unique offerings this cliffside town holds.

Shopping Delights

- **Local Crafts & Boutiques:** Wander through the charming streets lined with colorful shops. Discover handmade ceramics, hand-painted sandals, and locally woven textiles, each piece imbued with Positano's unique charm.

- **Linen Chic:** Immerse yourself in the "Positano style" with luxurious linen clothing and accessories. From breezy dresses to elegant tablecloths, find treasures crafted from the finest local linen.

- **Lemongrass Allure:** Embrace the Amalfi Coast's iconic citrus with lemon-infused souvenirs.

Discover handcrafted soaps, refreshing limoncello, and delectable pastries, each infused with the sunshine-kissed flavor of lemons.

- **Designer Delights:** Explore Positano's upscale boutiques showcasing renowned Italian and international brands. Treat yourself to designer fashion, jewelry, and accessories, adding a touch of luxury to your Positano experience.

Nightlife Gems
- **Sunset Aperitivo Ritual:** Experience the quintessential Positano evening. Sip on a refreshing cocktail or local wine as the sun dips below the horizon, painting the sky in fiery hues. Enjoy panoramic views from rooftop bars or charming piazzas, soaking in the vibrant atmosphere.

- **Live Music & Bars:** Immerse yourself in the lively Positano nightlife scene. Discover hidden bars with live music, trendy cocktail lounges, and authentic trattorias with buzzing energy, offering something for every taste and mood.

- Wine & Dine under the Stars: Savor a delicious meal at a waterfront restaurant as the stars begin to twinkle. Enjoy fresh seafood dishes, local specialties, and the gentle sea breeze, creating a truly romantic and unforgettable dining experience.

- Nightclubs & Beach Parties: For those seeking a more energetic experience, Positano offers nightclubs with live DJs and beach parties under the stars. Dance the night away with fellow travelers, enjoying the vibrant energy and stunning coastal backdrop.

Remember
- Many shops close for a midday break, typically between 1:00 PM and 4:00 PM.
- Bars and restaurants often stay open late, catering to the lively nightlife scene.

- Dress code varies depending on the venue, but generally, smart casual attire is appropriate.
- Embrace the relaxed Italian pace and enjoy the leisurely atmosphere, savoring the moment and connecting with the locals.

Additional Tips

- Consider learning a few basic Italian phrases to enhance your shopping and dining experiences.
- Barter is acceptable at some smaller shops, especially for local crafts and souvenirs.
- Pack comfortable shoes for navigating the hilly streets and stairs.
- Be prepared for crowds, especially during peak season. Arrive early or make reservations for popular restaurants and bars.

CHAPTER 6

Cetara & Vietri sul Mare

Beyond the bustling crowds of Positano and Amalfi, the Amalfi Coast holds two hidden gems waiting to be explored. Cetara and Vietri sul Mare. Each village offers a unique charm, captivating history, and delicious local flavors, promising an authentic Italian escape.

Cetara: A Fisherman's Paradise

Dive into Fishing Heritage: Nestled in a picturesque cove, Cetara boasts a centuries-old tradition of fishing and tuna processing. Explore the vibrant fish market, witness the ancient "tonnara" (tuna traps), and savor the freshest seafood dishes at waterfront restaurants.

Colatura di Alici: Cetara's culinary crown jewel is the "colatura di alici," a unique anchovy sauce produced using traditional methods. Taste its umami richness in pasta dishes, bruschetta, or simply drizzled on fresh bread.

Relax on the Beach: Unwind on the charming pebble beach, soak up the sunshine, and take a refreshing dip in the turquoise waters.

Wander the Labyrinthine Streets: Explore the narrow alleyways, discover hidden churches like San Pietro Apostolo, and admire the colorful houses adorned with bougainvillea flowers.

Vietri sul Mare: Where Art Meets the Coast
Colorful Ceramics Paradise: This charming village is renowned for its vibrant ceramic tradition. Wander through winding streets lined with colorful ceramic shops, marvel at handcrafted tableware, and witness artisans at work in their studios.

Museo della Ceramica: Delve deeper into the village's ceramic history at the Museo della

Ceramica, showcasing beautiful pottery collections and interactive exhibits.

Church of San Giovanni Battista: Witness the harmonious blend of architectural styles at the Church of San Giovanni Battista, featuring a majestic majolica-tiled dome.

Panoramic Views: Hike up to the Chiesa di San Martino for breathtaking views of the coastline, Capri Island, and the vibrant village below.

Relax on the Beach: Take a break on the small but scenic beach Marina di Vietri, perfect for swimming, sunbathing, and enjoying the laid-back atmosphere.

Connecting the Dots
Ferry Fun: Enjoy a scenic ferry ride between Cetara and Vietri sul Mare, offering stunning coastal views and a unique travel experience. The

journey takes only 5 minutes, making it a perfect way to explore both villages.

Path of the Gods: Embark on a challenging yet rewarding hike along the Path of the Gods, a scenic trail connecting Cetara and Positano. Witness breathtaking vistas, hidden coves, and charming villages along the way.

Planning Your Gemstone Exploration
Seasons: Spring (April-June) and autumn (September-October) offer pleasant weather and fewer crowds. July and August are peak season, with higher prices and larger crowds.

Getting Around: Both villages are walkable, but buses and taxis are available for exploring further areas. Consider purchasing a Campania Artecard for discounted entry to attractions and public transportation.

Accommodation: Choose from charming guesthouses, apartments, or nearby hotels in Positano or Amalfi.

Cetara and Vietri sul Mare offer an authentic Italian experience away from the crowds. Immerse yourself in their unique cultures, savor fresh seafood and local specialties, and create lasting memories amidst stunning coastal landscapes.

Exploring Cetara: The Tuna Capital

Nestled like a precious jewel along the Amalfi Coast, Cetara, Italy, isn't just a charming fishing village, it's the undisputed Tuna Capital of the country. Beyond its picturesque seaside setting and colorful houses cascading down cliffs, Cetara offers a unique cultural experience deeply rooted in the traditions of the sea and, of course, tuna. So, lace up your walking shoes, prepare to tantalize your taste buds, and dive into the heart of Cetara!

A Legacy Woven in Nets

Tonnara Tradition: Step back in time and discover the village's centuries-old "tonnara" (tuna traps). Witness the fascinating methods used to capture bluefin tuna during the traditional "mattanza" (slaughter), still practiced today with respect for sustainability.

Colatura di Alici: Cetara's culinary crown jewel is the "colatura di alici," an amber-colored anchovy sauce produced using ancient techniques. Savor its umami richness in pasta dishes, bruschetta, or simply drizzled on fresh bread.

Museo del Mare: Delve deeper into Cetara's maritime history at the Museo del Mare, showcasing traditional fishing tools, historical photos, and fascinating exhibits about the "tonnara" tradition.

A Feast for the Senses

Fresh Seafood Nirvana: Indulge in the freshest seafood dishes at waterfront restaurants overlooking the sparkling turquoise waters. From succulent tuna steaks to flavorful pasta with clams, prepare to be wowed by the bounty of the sea.

Beyond Tuna: While tuna takes center stage, Cetara's culinary scene offers more. Savor homemade pasta like "fusilli," explore local delicacies like "alici imbottite" (stuffed anchovies), and don't miss the sweet temptation of "sfogliatella," a flaky pastry filled with ricotta cream.

Cooking Class Immersion: Learn the secrets of Cetara cuisine firsthand by participating in a cooking class. Master the art of preparing "colatura di alici," cook traditional pasta dishes, and unveil the flavors of this unique culinary heritage.

Exploring Beyond the Plate

Charming Labyrinth: Wander through the village's narrow alleyways, adorned with vibrant flowers and colorful houses. Discover hidden piazzas, admire the 12th-century Chiesa di San Pietro Apostolo, and soak up the authentic Italian atmosphere.

Beach Bliss: Relax on the charming pebble beach, bask in the warm sunshine, and take a refreshing dip in the crystal-clear waters. Enjoy the laid-back atmosphere and stunning coastal views.

Planning Your Tuna-tastic Escape

Seasons: Spring (April-June) and autumn (September-October) offer pleasant weather and fewer crowds. July and August are peak season, with higher prices and larger crowds.

Getting Around: Cetara is a walkable village, but buses and taxis are available for exploring further areas. Consider purchasing a Campania Artecard for discounted entry to attractions and public transportation.

Accommodation: Choose from charming guesthouses, apartments, or nearby hotels in Positano or Amalfi.

Cetara is more than just a beautiful coastal village, it's an experience that lingers long after you leave. Immerse yourself in its rich maritime heritage, savor the mouthwatering flavors of the sea, and create unforgettable memories in this unique Tuna Capital of Italy.

Exploring Vietri sul Mare: Ceramics & Charm

Imagine a vibrant village nestled on the Amalfi Coast, where colorful houses cascade down cliffsides and the sound of ceramicists' chisels mingles with the gentle sea breeze. This is Vietri sul Mare, a charming gem renowned for its centuries-old tradition of ceramic craftsmanship and captivating Mediterranean allure. So, pack your wanderlust and prepare to be dazzled by Vietri's artistic spirit and coastal beauty!

Immerse Yourself in a Ceramic Wonderland
Stroll Through Living Galleries: Wander along winding streets transformed into open-air art galleries. Every corner boasts colorful ceramic shops showcasing exquisite tableware, decorative tiles, and handcrafted souvenirs. Witness skilled

artisans at work in their studios, and be mesmerized by the intricate details and vibrant colors.

Museo della Ceramica: Delve deeper into the village's ceramic legacy at the Museo della Ceramica. Explore an extensive collection showcasing ancient Etruscan pottery, contemporary masterpieces, and interactive exhibits that bring the art form to life.

Ceramic Painting Workshop: Unleash your inner artist by participating in a ceramic painting workshop. Learn traditional techniques, unleash your creativity on a piece of your own, and bring home a unique souvenir imbued with the spirit of Vietri.

Unveil the Village's Hidden Gems
Church of San Giovanni Battista: Witness the harmonious blend of architectural styles at the Church of San Giovanni Battista. Marvel at the

majestic majolica-tiled dome, intricate frescoes, and serene atmosphere.

Marina di Vietri: Take a break on the small but scenic beach. Relax on the sun-warmed pebbles, enjoy a refreshing dip in the turquoise waters, and soak up the laid-back Mediterranean vibes.

Chiesa di San Martino Hike: Embark on a challenging yet rewarding hike up to the Chiesa di San Martino. Witness breathtaking panoramic views of the coastline, Capri Island, and the colorful village nestled below.

Beyond the Village Charm

Explore Neighboring Gems: Take a scenic ferry ride to nearby Cetara, the Tuna Capital of Italy, and savor fresh seafood dishes or delve into its unique fishing heritage. Alternatively, visit the bustling Positano with its iconic cliffside houses and vibrant atmosphere.

Path of the Gods Hike: For the adventurous, embark on the legendary Path of the Gods, a challenging yet rewarding hike connecting Vietri sul Mare and Positano. Immerse yourself in breathtaking coastal scenery, hidden coves, and charming villages along the way.

Planning Your Artistic Escape

Seasons: Spring (April-June) and autumn (September-October) offer pleasant weather and fewer crowds. July and August are peak season, with higher prices and larger crowds.

Getting Around: Vietri sul Mare is walkable, but buses and taxis are available for exploring further areas. Consider purchasing a Campania Artecard for discounted entry to attractions and public transportation.

Accommodation: Choose from charming guesthouses, apartments, or nearby hotels in Positano or Amalfi.

Vietri sul Mare is more than just a picturesque village, it's an experience that ignites your senses and inspires creativity. Wander through living galleries, discover hidden gems, and immerse yourself in the village's artistic spirit.

CHAPTER 7

Ravello

Tucked away amidst the dramatic cliffs and verdant hills of the Amalfi Coast, lies the enchanting town of Ravello. While its neighbor Positano basks in the spotlight, Ravello offers a different kind of magic – a haven of serenity, cultural richness, and breathtaking beauty. Let this chapter be your guide to uncovering the hidden gems and unique experiences that await in this captivating town:

A Walk Through History

- **Duomo di Ravello:** Step back in time at the iconic Cathedral, a UNESCO World Heritage Site. Admire the intricate mosaics, Romanesque architecture, and the stunning Pulpit of Sant'Ambrogio, a masterpiece of Cosmatesque artistry.

- **Villa Rufolo:** Immerse yourself in the glamorous past at this historic villa. Explore the enchanting gardens overflowing with vibrant flowers, wander through the halls adorned with frescoes, and imagine the grand festivities hosted here for centuries.

- Museo della Carta (Paper Museum): Delve into the unique tradition of Amalfi paper, an art form celebrated for centuries. Learn about the intricate hand-beating methods, the use of local water sources, and the enduring legacy of Ravello's papermakers through interactive exhibits and historical displays.

Enthralling Gardens and Panoramic Vistas
- Giardini di Villa Cimbrone: Breathe in the fresh air and lose yourself in the mesmerizing beauty of these expansive gardens. Wander through rose-scented paths, discover hidden nooks with breathtaking views, and marvel at the iconic Terrace of Infinity, offering panoramic vistas of the Amalfi Coast.

- **Sentiero degli Dei (Path of the Gods):** Embark on a breathtaking hike along this legendary trail, offering awe-inspiring views of the coastline, hidden coves, and dramatic cliffs. Capture postcard-perfect moments, challenge yourself with scenic climbs, and connect with the natural beauty surrounding Ravello.

Art & Culture beyond Compare

- **Ravello Music Festival:** Immerse yourself in the town's vibrant artistic spirit during the renowned Ravello Music Festival. Witness world-renowned performers grace the stages in unique outdoor settings, creating an unforgettable cultural experience.

- **Art Galleries & Local Artisans:** Discover hidden gems showcasing the works of local and international artists. From charming galleries tucked away in narrow streets to artisan workshops crafting unique ceramics and jewelry, find treasures that capture the essence of Ravello's creativity.

Culinary Delights

- **Local Flavors with a View**: Savor fresh seafood dishes, homemade pasta specialties, and regional delicacies at restaurants boasting panoramic views. Enjoy the slow pace, embrace the Italian "dolce vita" lifestyle, and indulge in the freshest ingredients paired with stunning scenery.

- **Wine Tastings & Cooking Classes:** Embark on a sensory journey by joining a wine tasting or cooking class. Learn about local grape varieties, sample award-winning wines, and discover the secrets of preparing authentic Ravello dishes, creating memories that linger long after you leave.

Beyond the Sights

- **Wander the Labyrinthine Streets:** Get lost in the maze of narrow streets lined with pastel-colored houses, charming boutiques, and hidden piazzas. Embrace the slow pace, connect with friendly locals, and discover the hidden charm of Ravello's historic center.

- **Sunset Aperitivo Ritual:** Experience the quintessentially Italian tradition of enjoying a pre-dinner drink and nibbles while soaking in the breathtaking sunset views. Find a panoramic terrace, sip on a refreshing aperitivo, and savor the magical atmosphere.

Remember

- Ravello offers a more tranquil atmosphere compared to Positano. Embrace the quiet charm and slow pace of life.
- Consider purchasing a Campania Artecard for discounted entry to museums and public transportation.
- Comfortable shoes are essential for navigating the hilly streets and trails.
- Wear comfortable clothing and sun protection if planning outdoor activities.

Additional Tips

- Book accommodations in advance, especially during peak season.
- Learn a few basic Italian phrases to enhance your interactions with locals.
- Respect the local traditions and customs.
- Allow yourself to be captivated by the unique charm and beauty of Ravello, creating memories that will last a lifetime.

Gardens and villas

While the Amalfi Coast is renowned for its stunning coastline, Ravello offers a different kind of magic – a haven of verdant gardens and historic villas perched above it all. Prepare to be transported to a world of breathtaking beauty, fragrant blooms, and whispers of history as we explore Ravello's most captivating green spaces and majestic residences

Villa Cimbrone: An Ode to Romance and Infinity

- Terrace of Infinity: Undoubtedly the crown jewel, this iconic terrace offers unobstructed, panoramic views of the Amalfi Coast, stretching towards the endless horizon. Capture postcard-perfect photos and imagine yourself swept away by the breathtaking scenery.

Giardino della Principessa: Discover the "Garden of the Princess," a secluded oasis nestled within the walls of the Belmond Caruso Hotel. Stroll through its hidden nooks and crannies, each bursting with unique flora and offering intimate glimpses of the captivating coastline.

Valley of the Mills: Hike down the ancient path known as the "Valle delle Ferriere," once home to water-powered mills and now a lush green valley. Breathe in the fresh air, listen to the gentle murmur of streams, and be transported back in time amidst the ruins and natural beauty.

- **Garden of Wonders**: Wander through this enchanting maze of paths, discovering hidden nooks, whimsical sculptures, and vibrant flower beds bursting with roses, azaleas, and hydrangeas. Embrace the romantic atmosphere and lose yourself in the beauty.

- **Temple of Bacchus:** This charming folly offers a peaceful retreat adorned with statues and mosaics dedicated to the Roman god of wine. Enjoy a moment of serenity surrounded by greenery and imagine ancient celebrations held here.

Villa Rufolo: Whispers of Medieval Splendor

- **Gardens of Rufolo:** Immerse yourself in the timeless beauty of these terraced gardens, adorned with colorful flowers, citrus trees, and manicured hedges. Imagine medieval banquets held amidst the vibrant greenery and breathe in the fresh air.

- **Arab-Norman Hall:** Step back in time within this majestic hall, a magnificent example of architectural fusion featuring pointed arches, intricate mosaics, and stunning views.

- **Wagner's Grotto:** Immerse yourself in the legend of composer Richard Wagner, who found inspiration for "Parsifal" in this natural cave adorned with ancient statues and dripping ferns. Imagine the creative spark ignited by this unique setting.

Beyond the Big Two

- Giardino Rufolo a Ravello: Discover this hidden gem, often overshadowed by its larger neighbor. Explore its charming pathways, admire the blooming wisteria, and enjoy the panoramic views of the valley below.

- Villa Montuoro: Explore this charming 19th-century villa boasting lush gardens, a collection of citrus trees, and stunning views of the Amalfi Coast.

- Villa Episcopio: Enjoy a peaceful stroll through the gardens of this historic bishop's palace, offering a different perspective of Ravello's enchanting landscape.

Beyond the Gardens

Duomo di Ravello: Step back in time within the 11th-century Ravello Cathedral. Be mesmerized by the intricate details of its facade, wander through the serene interior adorned with mosaics, and soak in the rich history that resonates within its walls.

Wagner Festival: Immerse yourself in the cultural heart of Ravello by attending the renowned Wagner Festival. Held amidst this enchanting scenery, the festival celebrates classical music and the legacy of the renowned composer, creating an unforgettable experience.

Ceramics & Local Crafts: Discover the artistic spirit of Ravello by browsing local artisan shops. Find unique hand-painted ceramics, intricate embroidery, and handcrafted jewelry, each piece imbued with the character and traditions of this charming town.

Experiences for the Soul

Opera Under the Stars: Imagine the magic of witnessing an opera performance under the starlit sky of Ravello. Immerse yourself in the emotions of the music and the breathtaking setting, creating a memory that will forever be etched in your heart.

Private Balcony Sunset: Savor a delicious aperitivo on a private balcony overlooking the captivating coastline. As the sun dips below the horizon, painting the sky in hues of orange and pink, indulge in the moment and the unparalleled beauty that surrounds you.

Tips for the Perfect Garden Hopping Adventure

- Wear comfortable shoes for navigating the hilly paths and stairs.
- Purchase a Ravello Card for discounted entry to multiple gardens and villas.
- Pack a picnic lunch and enjoy a delightful break amidst the blooming beauty.
- Respect the gardens and villas, maintaining peace and quiet for all visitors.
- Allow yourself to be swept away by the enchanting atmosphere and create lasting memories of Ravello's verdant oasis.

Additional Tips

- Research opening hours and dress codes before visiting each garden or villa.
- Pack water and sunscreen, especially during hot summer days.
- Consider joining a guided tour for deeper insights into the history and architecture.
- Learn a few basic Italian phrases to enhance your interactions with locals.

Cultural events and festivals

Beyond its breathtaking landscapes and historical villas, Ravello pulsates with a vibrant cultural scene, offering a diverse range of events and festivals throughout the year. Prepare to immerse yourself in a tapestry of music, art, film, and local traditions that promise unforgettable experiences

Music for the Soul
- Ravello Music Festival (June-September): Witness world-renowned artists grace the stages of iconic outdoor settings like Villa Rufolo and Belvedere Principessa di Piemonte. From classical concerts to operatic performances under the starry sky, this prestigious festival is a must-see for music lovers.

- Concerti al Duomo (June-September): Enjoy intimate chamber music concerts held within the historic Ravello Cathedral. Revel in the acoustics of this sacred space and witness talented musicians perform classical masterpieces.

- **Ravello Jazz (July):** Immerse yourself in the rhythm of jazz in the enchanting setting of Villa Rufolo. Internationally renowned artists and emerging talents come together for an unforgettable musical celebration.

A Celebration of the Arts

- **Ravello Art (July-August):** Explore contemporary art exhibitions showcasing works by established and emerging Italian and international artists. Discover hidden galleries, participate in artist talks, and immerse yourself in the vibrant creative energy of Ravello.

- **Ravello Film Festival (October):** Indulge in your cinematic passion at this international film festival featuring screenings, dialogues with filmmakers, and workshops. Discover independent features, documentaries, and classic films in a breathtaking setting.

- Premio Letterario Città di Ravello (June): Celebrate literature at this prestigious award ceremony honoring Italian and international writers. Attend readings, book presentations, and discussions, and immerse yourself in the world of words.

Rooted in Tradition

- Corpus Domini Flower Carpet (June): Witness the artistic expression of devotion during this unique festival. The main square transforms into a stunning floral carpet depicting biblical scenes, created entirely from colorful petals.

- Festa della Madonna Addolorata (September): Experience the town's religious fervor during this traditional procession honoring the Virgin Mary. Immerse yourself in the spiritual atmosphere, witness the beautifully decorated streets, and join the local community in their celebration.

- Natale a Ravello (December): Immerse yourself in the festive spirit during Ravello's charming Christmas celebrations. Enjoy traditional Nativity scenes, carol performances, and local markets bustling with holiday cheer.

Tips for Embracing the Cultural Scene

- Purchase tickets in advance, especially for popular events like the Ravello Music Festival.
- Consider attending smaller, less crowded events for a more personal experience.
- Research dress codes for specific events, especially when attending religious celebrations.
- Embrace the opportunity to interact with locals and learn about their traditions.
- Be respectful of the cultural significance of each event and behave accordingly.

Additional Tips

- Download the official Ravello tourism app for event updates, schedules, and ticket information.
- Learn a few basic Italian phrases to enhance your communication and cultural understanding.
- Respect the local customs and traditions, especially during religious festivals.
- Consider combining your cultural experience with other activities like visiting historical sites or enjoying local gastronomy.

Exploring Minori: Lemons & Laid-Back Vibes

Step away from the bustling crowds and picture yourself strolling along a charming seaside promenade. Imagine the vibrant scent of lemons filling the air, the gentle lapping of waves against the shore, and the warm Italian sun caressing your skin. Welcome to Minori, a hidden gem along the Amalfi Coast where lemons zest the air and laid-back vibes reign supreme.

A Journey Through Sun-Kissed Charm

Beach Bliss: Unwind on Minori's longest beach, Marina di Minori. Sink your toes into the soft sand, cool off in the crystal-clear waters, and soak up the relaxed atmosphere. Rent a traditional striped umbrella and lose yourself in the rhythm of the waves.

Wander the Quaint Lanes: Immerse yourself in the heart of Minori by exploring its narrow, flower-adorned streets. Discover hidden piazzas where locals gather to chat, stumble upon charming artisan shops showcasing unique crafts, and savor the authentic Italian charm at every turn.

Limoncello Delights: Immerse yourself in the world of lemons, the lifeblood of Minori. Visit the historic Antica Dolceria Sal De Riso, renowned for its delectable limoncello cake and generations-old limoncello recipe. Savor the flavors, learn about the local production methods, and indulge in a truly sensorial experience.

Beyond the Usual

Roman Maritime Ruins: Unveil the fascinating history of Minori by exploring the archaeological site of the Villa Romana. Step back in time and imagine the lives of ancient Romans who once inhabited this seaside villa, adorned with mosaics and offering glimpses into their daily routines.

Path of Lemons: Embark on a scenic hike along the Sentiero dei Limoni, the "Path of Lemons."

Traverse lemon groves bursting with fragrant citrus fruits, enjoy panoramic views of the coastline, and discover hidden beaches like Cala Marina di Nova for a refreshing dip.

Culinary Delights: From fresh seafood pasta dishes to traditional Amalfi specialties, Minori's restaurants tantalize your taste buds. Enjoy a leisurely lunch on a terrace overlooking the sea, savor a romantic dinner under the stars, and discover the culinary traditions that define this charming town.

Experiences for the Soul

Cooking Class: Learn the art of preparing authentic Amalfi cuisine firsthand. In a local cooking class, master the art of making fresh pasta, whip up flavorful sauces, and learn the secrets of using local ingredients like lemons and fresh seafood.

Live Music & Local Events: Immerse yourself in the vibrant spirit of Minori by attending a live music performance in the piazza. Sway to the rhythm of traditional Neapolitan melodies, mingle with locals, and experience the warm hospitality that defines this community.

Boat Trip & Grotto Exploration: Embark on a boat tour along the rugged coastline and discover hidden gems like the Emerald Grotto. Witness the mesmerizing play of light on the water as sunlight filters through the underwater cave, creating an ethereal spectacle.

Remember
- Minori is easily accessible by public transportation or car.
- Wear comfortable shoes as the town involves some walking.
- Pack light clothing and swimwear for enjoying the beach and exploring the surroundings.
- Embrace the slower pace of life and savor the simple pleasures of this charming town.

Recommended Itineraries

Whether you crave cultural immersion, historical exploration, or simply relaxation amidst vibrant gardens, the town caters to diverse interests. Let's delve into three itinerary options to guide your Ravello adventure.

1. History Buff's Delight (2-3 days)

Day 1

- **Morning:** Immerse yourself in the grandeur of Villa Rufolo, exploring its gardens, Arab-Norman Hall, and Wagner's Grotto. Imagine medieval banquets held within its walls.

- **Afternoon:** Wander through the historic center, browsing charming shops and admiring the Duomo di Ravello, adorned with Romanesque architecture and mosaics.

- **Evening:** Enjoy a traditional dinner at a restaurant boasting panoramic views, savoring local delicacies and soaking in the sunset atmosphere.

Day 2

- **Morning:** Delve into the history of papermaking at the Museo della Carta. Learn about the unique crafting process and witness the vibrant local tradition.

- **Afternoon:** Hike along the Path of the Gods, experiencing breathtaking coastal views and hidden coves. Capture scenic moments and connect with nature.

- **Evening:** Attend a classical music concert at the Concerti al Duomo, immersing yourself in the acoustics and intimate setting of the Ravello Cathedral.

Day 3 (optional)

- **Morning:** Explore the enchanting gardens of Villa Cimbrone. Wander through the Garden of Wonders, marvel at the iconic Terrace of Infinity, and capture postcard-perfect photos.

- **Afternoon:** Travel to nearby Pompeii or Herculaneum, stepping back in time to explore the fascinating ruins of these ancient Roman cities.

2. Art & Culture Enthusiast's Journey (2-3 days)

Day 1
- **Morning:** Discover contemporary art at the Ravello Art exhibition, exploring works by established and emerging artists. Engage in dialogues and delve into the creative energy of the town.

- **Afternoon:** Attend a film screening or workshop at the Ravello Film Festival, immersing yourself in the world of cinema and discovering captivating stories.

Day 2
- **Morning:** Visit the Museo Correale, housing an impressive collection of Neapolitan art and archaeological artifacts, offering a glimpse into the region's rich history.

- **Afternoon:** Attend a performance at the Ravello Music Festival, experiencing world-class artists grace the stage in unique outdoor settings. Immerse yourself in the magical atmosphere.

Day 3 (optional)
- **Morning:** Explore the charming Giardino Rufolo, a hidden gem boasting fragrant wisteria and panoramic views. Enjoy a peaceful retreat amidst its lush greenery.

- **Afternoon:** Embark on a cultural walking tour, delving into Ravello's history, architectural gems, and local traditions. Connect with a knowledgeable guide and gain deeper insights.

3. Relaxation & Nature Lover's Escape (2-3 days)

Day 1
- **Morning:** Unwind in the tranquil Giardini di Villa Cimbrone, soaking in the breathtaking views and exploring hidden nooks. Breathe in the fresh air and embrace the serenity.

- **Afternoon:** Enjoy a relaxing afternoon at a beach club in nearby Amalfi or Maiori, sunbathing, swimming in the turquoise waters, and indulging in fresh seafood.

Day 2
- **Morning:** Participate in a cooking class, learning the secrets of preparing authentic Ravello dishes and regional specialties. Savor your creations for lunch, enjoying the local culinary heritage.

- **Afternoon:** Embark on a boat tour along the Amalfi Coast, discovering hidden coves, secluded beaches, and dramatic cliffs from a unique perspective. Take a refreshing dip in the crystal-clear waters.

Day 3 (optional)
- **Morning:** Wander through the picturesque streets of Ravello, discovering hidden piazzas, charming cafes, and local artisans showcasing their crafts. Embrace the slow pace and connect with friendly locals.

- **Afternoon:** Rejuvenate with a spa treatment at a luxury hotel, indulging in massages, facials, or personalized wellness experiences. Relax your mind and body, letting the tranquility of Ravello wash over you.

CHAPTER 8

Capri

Perched atop dramatic cliffs overlooking the sparkling turquoise waters of the Mediterranean, is more than just a stunning island destination, it's an experience for the senses. From its glamorous piazzas and colorful houses cascading down cliffs to its hidden coves and breathtaking panoramic views, Capri exudes an enchanting charm that has captivated visitors for centuries.

Capri at a Glance

- **Location:** Campania region, southern Italy, near the Sorrento Peninsula
- **Size:** 4 square miles (10 square kilometers)
- **Population:** Approximately 14,000 residents
- **Language:** Italian, although English is widely spoken in tourist areas
- **Currency:** Euro (€)

- **Best time to visit:** April to June and September to October (avoid the crowds of July and August)

Captivating Sights and Experiences

1. Wander Through the Picturesque Piazzas
- **Piazzetta Umberto I:** The heart of Capri, this bustling square is lined with designer boutiques, charming cafes, and vibrant restaurants. Soak in the atmosphere, people-watch, and enjoy a cup of espresso while basking in the Italian sunshine.

- **Piazza della Pace:** Offering panoramic views of the Faraglioni rock formations and the endless horizon, this peaceful square is a perfect spot for relaxation and capturing stunning photos.

2. Explore the Breathtaking Grottos
- **Grotta Azzurra (Blue Grotto):** Take a small boat into this natural wonder, where sunlight filters through an underwater cave entrance, illuminating

the water with an ethereal blue glow. Witness the mesmerizing effect and capture unforgettable moments.

- **Grotta Verde (Green Grotto):** Accessible by swimming or boat, this underwater cave features emerald-green waters reflecting the sunlight, creating a magical atmosphere.

3. Hike Along Scenic Trails

- **Path of the Gods:** Embark on a challenging yet rewarding hike along this legendary trail, offering breathtaking panoramas of the coastline, hidden coves, and dramatic cliffs. Capture postcard-perfect moments and connect with nature.

- **Via Tragara:** Stroll along this panoramic walkway, admiring the Faraglioni rocks, colorful houses clinging to the cliffs, and the vast expanse of the Mediterranean Sea.

4. Relax on Pristine Beaches

- **Marina Grande:** This larger beach offers a mix of relaxation and watersports, with sun loungers, restaurants, and opportunities for kayaking and stand-up paddleboarding.

- **Marina Piccola:** Reachable by boat or a steep walk down from Capri town, this charming cove offers crystal-clear waters, a relaxing atmosphere, and stunning views.

5. Immerse Yourself in History and Culture

- **Augustus Gardens:** These lush gardens offer a tranquil escape with sculptures, fountains, and panoramic views. Imagine ancient Roman emperors strolling through these grounds.

- **Certosa di San Giacomo:** Explore this 14th-century monastery, admiring its architectural details, cloisters, and beautiful majolica tile works.

Beyond the Sights

- Indulge in Local Delicacies: Savor fresh seafood dishes, homemade pasta specialties, and regional treats like caprese salad and limoncello. Don't miss the opportunity to try the island's unique Capri DOP extra virgin olive oil.

- Experience the "Dolce Vita": Embrace the Italian slow pace of life, enjoy leisurely meals with delicious food and conversation, and soak up the warm sunshine and vibrant atmosphere.

- Shop for Unique Souvenirs: From handcrafted sandals and limoncello to designer clothing and local ceramics, find treasures that capture the essence of Capri.

- Perfumary Workshop: Inhale the essence of Capri in a fragrance creation workshop. Blend essential oils, experiment with scents, and bottle your own personalized perfume, capturing the island's aroma.

Remember

- Wear comfortable shoes for navigating the hilly streets and stairs.
- Consider purchasing a Campania Artecard for discounted entry to museums and public transportation.
- Be prepared for crowds, especially during peak season. Book accommodations and reservations in advance.
- Respect the local environment and follow sustainable practices while exploring the beaches and natural areas.
- Embrace the "dolce vita" lifestyle and savor the beauty and tranquility of Capri's unique offerings.

Additional Tips

- Learn a few basic Italian phrases to enhance your interaction with locals.

- Pack sunscreen, sunglasses, and a hat for sunny days.

- Consider joining a guided tour to gain deeper insights into Capri's history and culture.

- Relax and enjoy the island's unique charm, Capri is a place to create lasting memories.

Exploring Capri: La Dolce Vita at its Finest

Imagine yourself sailing past iconic rock formations bathed in golden sunlight, the scent of lemons mingling with the salty air. Envision vibrant piazzas buzzing with life, and charming streets lined with designer boutiques. Welcome to Capri, where every corner whispers tales of Hollywood glamour and the Italian art of living well.

Immerse Yourself in "La Dolce Vita"

Piazzetta Capris & Via Camerelle: Mingle with celebrities and locals alike at the legendary Piazzetta. Sip your morning espresso while watching the world go by, indulge in designer shopping along Via Camerelle, and feel the pulse of Capri's vibrant heart.

Faraglioni Rocks & Grotta Azzurra: Embark on a boat tour and marvel at the majestic Faraglioni rock formations rising from the sea. Witness the natural wonder of the Arch, then enter the ethereal

Blue Grotto, where sunlight paints the water an enchanting blue.

Chairlift to Mount Solaro: Ascend to the summit and be rewarded with breathtaking panoramic views encompassing the entire island, the Sorrento Peninsula, and even Naples on a clear day. Savor the fresh air and feel the accomplishment of reaching the top.

Beyond the Glamorous Facade

Hidden Coves & Secluded Beaches: Escape the crowds and discover hidden gems like Marina Piccola and Cala Marina Grande, accessible only by boat or footpaths. Relax on pebbled shores, swim in crystal-clear waters, and find your own slice of paradise.

Anacapri & Villa San Michele: Explore the charming village of Anacapri, known for its peaceful atmosphere and colorful houses. Discover the whimsical Villa San Michele, built by Swedish physician Axel Munthe, and be captivated by its unique architecture and stunning gardens.

Indulge in Culinary Delights

Fresh Seafood & Caprese Salad: Savor the freshest seafood pasta dishes, bursting with the flavors of the Mediterranean. Savor the iconic Caprese salad, a simple yet perfect combination of ripe tomatoes, creamy mozzarella, and fragrant basil.

Lemons & Limoncello: Immerse yourself in the island's signature citrus experience. Visit a local limoncello producer and learn about the traditional production methods. Sample different varieties and indulge in the refreshing flavor of this iconic liqueur.

Panoramic Dining: Experience "La Dolce Vita" at its finest by dining on a terrace overlooking the sea. Savor delicious cuisine amidst breathtaking views, creating memories that will linger long after your return.

Tips for an Unforgettable Journey

- Capri is car-free, so explore by foot, taxi, or funicular.
- Purchase a Campania Artecard for discounted entry to museums and attractions.
- Pack comfortable shoes and light clothing for exploring the island's hills and beaches.
- Embrace the slower pace of life and savor the moment.

Capri Town & Marina Grande

While Capri Town, perched high on the cliffs, exudes an air of sophistication, Marina Grande, the island's main port, pulsates with a vibrant energy. Exploring both towns allows you to experience the diverse facets of Capri's magic.

Capri Town: Where Luxury Meets History

Certosa di San Giacomo: A 14th-century monastery known for its majolica floor tiles and peaceful cloister. Immerse yourself in the spiritual atmosphere and admire the artwork.

Marina Grande: Where Tradition Meets the Sea

Marina: The lively harbor, bustling with colorful fishing boats, ferries, and yachts. Arrive in style or embark on a boat tour around the island.

Migliera: A scenic coastal path offering stunning views of the Faraglioni rocks and the coastline. Hike or walk, enjoying the sea breeze and the natural beauty.

Bagni di Tiberio: Roman imperial ruins perched on the cliffs, offering archaeological treasures and panoramic views. Explore the site and imagine the grandeur of the past.

Planning Your Visit

Getting there: Take a ferry from Naples, Sorrento, or Amalfi.

Getting around: Capri Town is pedestrian-only, so explore on foot, take the funicular railway, or hire a taxi. Marina Grande is accessible by car, but parking can be challenging.

Accommodation: Choose from a variety of hotels, villas, and guesthouses in both Capri Town and Marina Grande, depending on your budget and preferences.

Best time to visit: Spring (April-May) and autumn (September-October) offer pleasant weather and fewer crowds. July and August are peak season, with higher prices and larger crowds.

Insider Tips

- Purchase a Campania Artecard for discounted entry to museums and attractions.
- Pack comfortable shoes for walking and exploring.
- Be prepared for crowds, especially in the peak season.
- Embrace the slower pace of life and enjoy the relaxed atmosphere.

With its vibrant atmosphere, rich history, and stunning natural beauty, Capri Town and Marina Grande offer an unforgettable experience for any traveler. !

Anacapri & Monte Solaro

Capri isn't just about the bustling Piazzetta and glamorous Marina Grande. Venture beyond the crowds and discover Anacapri, a village of serene charm, and Monte Solaro, the island's majestic peak. Here's your guide to escaping the hustle and reveling in breathtaking views and hidden gems.

Anacapri: Where Peace Reigns

Piazza Capriccio: The charming heart of Anacapri, adorned with flowers and vibrant houses. Enjoy a gelato, linger at a cafe, and soak in the tranquil atmosphere.

Casa Rossa: Axel Munthe's whimsical former home, now a museum showcasing his life and eclectic collection. Explore the colorful rooms and gardens, feeling transported to a different era.

Church of San Michele: A 16th-century church featuring colorful majolica tiles and stunning views.

Appreciate the intricate artwork and enjoy the peaceful ambiance.

Local Crafts & Boutiques: Discover unique hand-painted ceramics, colorful limoncello bottles, and other delightful souvenirs in charming local shops.

Monte Solaro: Conquering the Summit for Panoramic Rewards

Chairlift Ride: Ascend to the peak aboard the scenic chairlift, enjoying breathtaking views of the coastline, Faraglioni rocks, and surrounding islands.

Panoramic Views: Once at the top, be rewarded with 360-degree vistas encompassing Capri, the Sorrento Peninsula, and even Naples on a clear day. Capture stunning photos and soak in the grandeur.

Walks & Hikes: Explore further by following scenic trails leading to hidden viewpoints or the

Hermitage of Cetrella, a charming church nestled on the slopes.

Restaurant & Bar: Enjoy refreshing drinks and light meals at the summit restaurant while marveling at the panoramic backdrop.

Planning Your Visit

Getting there: Take a bus or taxi from Capri Town or Marina Grande. Consider walking for a scenic experience (around 1 hour).

Ticket options: Purchase a combined ticket for the chairlift and Casa Rossa for a discounted rate.

Comfortable shoes: Wear footwear suitable for walking on uneven terrain, especially if planning to hike.

Sun protection: Pack sunscreen and a hat for the exposure at the summit.

Timing: Go early in the morning or late afternoon to avoid crowds, especially during peak season.

Insider Tips

- **Consider a guided tour:** Learn fascinating historical anecdotes and gain insights into local life.
- **Sample local specialties:** Enjoy a picnic lunch with Caprese salad, fresh seafood dishes, or homemade limoncello at the summit restaurant.
- **Relax at the Belvedere:** Rest your legs and admire the scenic landscape from a shaded viewing platform.

Embrace the slower pace of Anacapri and the thrilling ascent to Monte Solaro. Unwind amidst charming local vibes, capture breathtaking panoramas, and create memories that will last a lifetime. Your Capri adventure awaits!

Grotto Azzurra & Faraglioni Rocks

Capri, the island jewel of the Mediterranean, boasts not only glamorous piazzas and charming villages, but also natural wonders that leave visitors awestruck. Among these marvels are the Grotto Azzurra (Blue Grotto), a mystical cave illuminated by an ethereal blue light, and the Faraglioni Rocks, imposing rock formations rising dramatically from the sea. Get ready to embark on a journey to these captivating landmarks!

Grotto Azzurra: Where Sunlight Paints the Water Blue

Imagine entering a cave, sunlight filtering through an underwater opening, casting an enchanting blue glow on the water. This is the magic of the Grotto Azzurra, a natural phenomenon accessible only by small rowboats. As you enter the grotto, be mesmerized by the ethereal blue light reflecting off the water, creating an almost dreamlike atmosphere.

Things to Know

Entrance: Only small rowboats can enter the grotto, so expect a wait during peak season. Tickets are purchased on-site.

Experience: The boat ride inside the grotto is short, lasting around 5 minutes. However, the memory of the unique blue light will stay with you forever.

Best time to visit: Early morning or late afternoon when the sunlight hits the water at the right angle, maximizing the blue effect.

Photography: Taking photos inside the grotto is challenging due to low light. Consider purchasing official photos taken by local boatmen.

Faraglioni Rocks: Where Nature Sculpts the Coastline

Standing tall off the coast of Capri are the Faraglioni Rocks, three majestic rock formations sculpted by wind and waves over millennia. These natural wonders come in different sizes and shapes, with the largest one even featuring a natural archway.

Things to Know

Best views: Admire the Faraglioni from various angles: by boat, from the Punta Tragara viewpoint in Capri Town, or from the Belvedere della Migliera in Marina Grande.

Boat tours: Embark on a boat tour around the island for a closer look at the Faraglioni and other hidden coves.

Snorkeling and Diving: Explore underwater worlds teeming with colorful fish, coral reefs, and shipwrecks. Discover underwater grottos and marvel at the vibrant marine life of the Mediterranean Sea.

Legend: Local legend has it that jumping off the Faraglioni brings good luck, but swimming near them is prohibited due to safety reasons.

Beyond the Sights

Combine your visit: Include both the Grotto Azzurra and the Faraglioni in a boat tour, enjoying the convenience and stunning coastal views along the way.

Relaxation: After your exploration, unwind on a nearby beach, soaking up the sunshine and the turquoise waters.

Local Flavors: Savor a delicious seafood lunch or indulge in a refreshing gelato while enjoying the views of the Faraglioni or the Capri coastline.

Remember

- Wear comfortable shoes and clothing suitable for exploring uneven terrain and potentially hot weather.

- Sun protection is essential, especially when spending time on the boat or near the water.
- Pack a light sweater or jacket as the temperature can drop slightly inside the Grotto Azzurra.
- Embrace the beauty of these natural wonders and respect the environment while exploring them.

With their unique charm and enchanting beauty, the Grotto Azzurra and the Faraglioni Rocks are must-sees for any visitor to Capri. Let these natural wonders add a touch of magic to your island adventure!

Shopping and dining experiences

Capri isn't just a feast for the eyes, it's a delightful experience for your taste buds and shopping spree dreams. From designer boutiques to hidden trattorias, the island offers a unique blend of luxury and authentic charm.

Shop Like a Star

- Piazzetta Umberto I: The heart of Capri's shopping scene, this iconic square boasts designer flagships like Dior, Fendi, and Prada. Indulge in window-shopping or treat yourself to a piece of high fashion.

- Via Camerelle: A labyrinthine network of narrow streets, this area offers a mix of local and international boutiques, trendy clothing stores, and artisan workshops showcasing handcrafted leather goods, ceramics, and limoncello.

- Corso Giacomo Matteotti: Find upscale boutiques and art galleries alongside traditional shops selling Capri sandals, handcrafted jewelry, and locally made souvenirs.

Dine with a View

- **Ristorante La Capannina:** Nestled amidst fragrant gardens, this Michelin-starred restaurant offers refined Italian cuisine with breathtaking panoramas of the Faraglioni rocks.

- **Da Tonino:** A local favorite, this trattoria serves up classic Caprese dishes like spaghetti alle vongole (clams) and fresh fish in a lively atmosphere overlooking the Marina Grande.

- **Il Riccio:** Perched on a cliff overlooking the sea, this Michelin-starred restaurant offers a luxurious dining experience with innovative seafood dishes and unparalleled views.

- **Ristorante La Fontelina:** Enjoy fresh seafood pasta and breathtaking scenery at this iconic cliffside restaurant accessible only by boat.

Beyond the Boutiques and Michelin Stars

- **Local Markets:** Immerse yourself in the daily life and flavors of Capri at the farmers market in the Piazzetta or the fish market in Marina Grande. Sample local cheeses, fresh fruits, and homemade limoncello.

- **Gelato Degustation:** No Italian vacation is complete without gelato! Indulge in creamy scoops and unique flavors at cafes like Buonocore or Rhum Bar.

- **Picnic under the Sun:** Pick up fresh bread, cheese, salami, and local wine from a deli and enjoy a picnic with stunning views at the Giardini di Augusto or Marina Piccola.

Insider Tips

- Be prepared for high prices, especially in designer stores and waterfront restaurants.

- Consider booking reservations for popular restaurants in advance, especially during peak season.
- Look for hidden trattorias and family-run cafes for authentic dishes and affordable prices.
- Learn a few basic Italian phrases to enhance your interaction with locals.
- Carry reusable bags to avoid plastic shopping bags and respect the environment.

Capri's culinary and shopping scene is an extension of its unique charm. Indulge in the experience, savor the flavors, and let the island's beauty inspire your purchases. Remember, the memories you create and the connections you forge are the true treasures you'll take home.

CHAPTER 9

Naples

The vibrant capital of southern Italy, is a city that throws its arms around you, enveloping you in its rich history, delectable cuisine, and captivating chaos. From ancient Roman ruins to world-renowned pizzas, Naples offers an unforgettable experience for every traveler.

Immerse Yourself in History

Castel Nuovo: Explore this imposing medieval fortress, offering panoramic city views and fascinating exhibits on Neapolitan history.

Pompeii & Herculaneum: Step back in time and witness the haunting beauty of these ancient Roman cities, frozen in time by the eruption of Mount Vesuvius.

Tarantella Dance Lesson: Immerse yourself in the lively spirit of Southern Italy, learning the energetic steps and vibrant rhythms of the traditional Tarantella dance.

Indulge in Culinary Delights

Pizza Nirvana: Savor the original Neapolitan pizza, made with simple, fresh ingredients and cooked in wood-fired ovens. From the classic Margherita to the adventurous salsiccia e friarielli, there's a pizza for every taste.

Street Food Delights: Explore the vibrant street food scene, trying fried pizzas (pizza fritta), pasta fritta, and other local specialties.

Coffee Culture: Immerse yourself in the city's iconic coffee culture, savoring a strong espresso or creamy cappuccino at a local cafe.

Seafood Heaven: Enjoy the freshest seafood dishes, from pasta alle vongole (clams) to frittura mista (mixed fried fish), overlooking the stunning waterfront.

Embrace the Chaos

Explore the Quartieri Spagnoli: This historic district, once known for its rough reputation, offers a glimpse into traditional Neapolitan life with its lively markets and friendly locals.

Witness the Passion: Be swept away by the Neapolitans' fervent passion for football, especially if you manage to catch a game at the iconic Stadio San Paolo.

Jetski Adventure: Thrill-seekers can zip across the Bay of Naples, experiencing the exhilaration of high-speed rides and enjoying unique views of the coastline.

Take it Slow: Embrace the Neapolitan pace of life, where time seems to bend and schedules are more of a suggestion. Relax at a cafe, people-watch in the piazzas, and soak up the unique atmosphere.

Planning Your Visit

Getting there: Naples has an international airport and is well-connected by train to other Italian cities.

Getting around: The city center is walkable, but public transportation is available, including metro, buses, and funiculars.

Accommodation: Choose from a variety of hotels, guesthouses, and apartments to suit your budget and preferences.

Best time to visit: Spring (April-June) and autumn (September-October) offer pleasant weather and fewer crowds. July and August are peak season, with higher prices and larger crowds.

Insider Tips

- Purchase a Campania Artecard for discounted entry to museums and attractions.
- Pack comfortable shoes for walking on uneven terrain.

- Be prepared for crowds, especially in popular tourist areas.
- Learn a few basic Italian phrases to enhance your experience.
- Don't be afraid to ask locals for recommendations on hidden gems and authentic experiences.

With its rich history, mouthwatering cuisine, and captivating chaos, Naples is a city that will stay with you long after you leave.

Museums and historical sites

Naples, Italy, isn't just a vibrant city with delicious pizza and stunning vistas, it's a living museum brimming with history and culture. From ancient Roman relics to opulent royal palaces, delve into the past through these diverse museums and historical sites:

For the Archaeology Enthusiast

Naples Archaeological Museum: Immerse yourself in the world of Pompeii and Herculaneum, with an extensive collection of frescoes, mosaics, and everyday objects unearthed from these tragic cities frozen in time. Marvel at the intricate details and imagine the lives they once belonged to.

MANN - National Archaeological Museum of Naples: Explore a wider range of ancient treasures, including Egyptian artifacts, Greek sculptures, and stunning Roman mosaics. Get a comprehensive understanding of the Mediterranean's rich history across different civilizations.

Catacombs of San Gennaro: Descend beneath the vibrant city and explore these labyrinthine tunnels, originally used as early Christian burial grounds. Admire the early Christian artwork and learn about the fascinating legends of Saint Gennaro.

For the Art Lover

Galleria Umberto I: This majestic 19th-century shopping arcade is a work of art itself, adorned with intricate glass ceilings and marble floors. Immerse yourself in the luxurious atmosphere while browsing high-end boutiques and sipping coffee in historic cafes.

Museo Nazionale di Capodimonte: Nestled within a royal palace, this museum houses an impressive collection of Italian art, ranging from Renaissance masterpieces by Botticelli and Caravaggio to Neapolitan paintings and contemporary works. Get lost in the beauty and diverse expressions.

Cappella Sansevero: Witness the breathtaking Veiled Christ sculpture, known for its hauntingly realistic depiction of a shrouded figure. Admire the other intricate marble sculptures and the eerie anatomical models displayed in the chapel.

For the History Buff

Royal Palace of Naples: Step into the opulent life of the Bourbon kings by exploring this grand palace, showcasing luxurious halls, lavishly decorated rooms, and stunning art collections. Imagine royal banquets and courtly intrigues set against this magnificent backdrop.

Castel Nuovo (Maschio Angioino): This imposing medieval fortress offers stunning views of the city and harbor. Explore its halls, courtyards, and exhibitions showcasing the city's turbulent history from the Angevin dynasty to the Spanish rule.

Naples Underground (Napoli Sotterranea): Embark on a guided tour through the hidden network of tunnels beneath the city, used for various purposes throughout history. Learn about aqueducts, bomb shelters, and even early Christian communities in this subterranean world.

Bonus

Spaccanapoli: Wander through this historic center, lined with baroque churches, Renaissance palaces, and vibrant street art. Soak in the architectural styles and historical significance of each building, imagining the stories they hold.

Naples Bay Cruise: Sail around the Bay of Naples, admiring the stunning skyline of the city, Mount Vesuvius, and historic landmarks like Castel dell'Ovo. Enjoy panoramic views, swimming breaks, and insights from knowledgeable guides.

Mount Vesuvius: For a historical and natural experience, hike or take a tour to the crater of Mount Vesuvius, the volcano responsible for

Pompeii's tragic fate. Stand in awe of its power and gain insights into the devastating eruption.

Tips

- Purchase a Campania Artecard for discounted entry to many museums and public transportation.
- Consider guided tours for deeper insights and historical context.
- Explore during off-peak hours to avoid crowds, especially in popular sites.
- Dress comfortably for walking and exploring historical sites.

Enjoy your journey through Naples' rich history and let these museums and historical sites paint a vivid picture of its fascinating past!

Shopping & Dining

Naples, the vibrant heart of southern Italy, offers more than just ancient ruins and mouthwatering pizzas. From bustling markets overflowing with fresh produce to hidden boutiques showcasing local craftsmanship, and from cozy trattorias to Michelin-starred restaurants, the city caters to every shopper and diner's desires.

Shopping Delights

Spaccanapoli: Wander through this historic center, where artisan workshops and trendy stores share space with traditional family-run businesses. Discover hand-painted ceramics, intricately crafted leather goods, and unique Neapolitan souvenirs.

San Gregorio Armeno: Immerse yourself in the Christmas spirit year-round! This narrow street is famous for its nativity scene figurines, handcrafted with meticulous detail.

Via Toledo: Indulge in some high-end retail therapy along this iconic avenue. Explore flagship stores of international brands alongside elegant local boutiques.

Pignasecca Market: Dive into the bustling atmosphere of this traditional market. Haggle for the freshest fruits and vegetables, local cheeses and cured meats, and handmade pasta specialties.

Antignano Flea Market: Unearth hidden treasures at this sprawling flea market held every Sunday. Find vintage clothing, antique furniture, quirky collectibles, and unique art pieces.

Local Markets

A Sensory Overload: Immerse yourself in the sights, smells, and sounds of traditional Neapolitan markets. Explore the Mercato di Porta Nolana, a colorful haven of fresh produce, regional specialties, and handcrafted goods. Haggle with friendly vendors and discover hidden gems like local cheeses, cured meats, and homemade limoncello.

Dining Adventures

Pizzerias: Explore iconic pizzerias like Starita a Materdei or Da Michele for an authentic experience.

Trattorias: Immerse yourself in the warmth of traditional Neapolitan hospitality. Enjoy hearty pasta dishes like ragù or spaghetti alle vongole, fresh seafood specialties, and flavorful regional wines.

Michelin-starred: Treat yourself to an unforgettable culinary journey at one of Naples' renowned Michelin-starred restaurants. Experience innovative interpretations of Neapolitan cuisine with stunning views and impeccable service.

Tips & Recommendations

Bargaining: Don't be afraid to bargain at markets and flea markets. It's part of the local culture, and you can score great deals!

Cash: While many places accept credit cards, having some cash on hand is always helpful, especially at markets and smaller shops.

Opening Hours: Shops typically open late in the morning and close for a long lunch break. Restaurants often have late dinner hours, so don't worry about rushing dinner.

Hidden Gems: Seek out recommendations from locals for hidden trattorias, artisan workshops, and charming cafes off the beaten path.

Seasonal Specialties: Embrace the seasonal flavors! Enjoy fresh peaches and tomatoes in summer, and indulge in hearty pasta dishes with truffles in the fall.

Whether you seek unique handcrafted souvenirs or crave an authentic culinary adventure, Naples offers endless possibilities. So, open your senses, wander the streets, and discover the hidden gems that this captivating city has to offer!

CHAPTER 10

Pompeii

Pompeii, Italy, isn't just an archaeological site, it's a window into a bustling Roman city tragically preserved by the eruption of Mount Vesuvius in 79 AD. Wandering through its eerily silent streets, frozen in time, offers a poignant glimpse into everyday life centuries ago. Prepare to be captivated by the haunting beauty and historical significance of this UNESCO World Heritage Site.

Stepping Back in Time

Imagine walking down cobbled streets lined with shops and houses, their facades adorned with colorful frescoes. Picture the bustling marketplace, the echoing sounds of the public baths, and the laughter of children playing in the piazza. Pompeii was a vibrant city frozen in time, offering a unique perspective on Roman life, culture, and architecture.

Eerie Echoes of the Past

Explore the haunting remnants of homes, businesses, and public spaces, remarkably preserved by ash and pumice. Peer into kitchens with utensils still on tables, bakeries with loaves of bread carbonized in ovens, and temples where statues stand guard in eternal silence. Imagine the lives interrupted, the stories untold, and the final moments of a city forever etched in ash.

Unveiling Daily Life

Beyond the grand structures, Pompeii reveals the details of everyday life. Discover well-preserved bathhouses with changing rooms, pools, and saunas. Visit houses adorned with elaborate mosaics and frescoes depicting mythological scenes and daily activities. Witness the ingenious Roman engineering system of aqueducts and sewers, still visible today.

The Power of Nature

Mount Vesuvius, once a seemingly peaceful mountain, transformed into a destructive force in 79 AD. Explore the casts of victims, their expressions forever etched in agony, a stark reminder of the volcano's devastating power. Visit the amphitheater, now filled with volcanic ash, and imagine the terror and chaos that unfolded as the eruption commenced.

Beyond the Ruins

Enhance your Pompeii experience by visiting the Antiquarium, showcasing artifacts unearthed from the city. Delve deeper into the history at the National Archaeological Museum of Naples, housing impressive collections of Pompeii treasures. Don't miss the Garden of the Fugitives, offering a poignant glimpse into the final moments of some Pompeii residents.

Tips for Your Visit
- Wear comfortable shoes for walking on uneven terrain.

- Purchase your tickets in advance, especially during peak season.
- Consider a guided tour for deeper insights and historical context.
- Bring sunscreen, a hat, and water, as shade is limited.
- Respect the site and artifacts, and avoid touching or removing anything.

Pompeii isn't just a collection of ruins, it's a powerful reminder of the fragility of life and the enduring power of history. Let your visit be a journey through time, sparking your imagination and leaving you with a deeper appreciation for the past.

Archaeological site details

Pompeii, Italy, isn't just a UNESCO World Heritage Site, it's a portal to the past, a frozen-in-time Roman city offering an unparalleled glimpse into daily life two millennia ago. As you wander through its eerily silent streets and explore its excavated structures, each detail whispers stories of a vibrant community tragically lost to the eruption of Mount Vesuvius in 79 AD. Here's a closer look at some key archaeological details that will enrich your Pompeian exploration:

Public Spaces

Forum: The heart of Pompeii's public life, the Forum was a bustling marketplace and gathering place. Admire the Temple of Jupiter, the Basilica (administrative building), and the Macellum (covered market).

Amphitheater: Witness the impressive remains of this 20,000-seat venue, used for gladiatorial combats and public performances. Imagine the roar of the crowd echoing through the stands.

Stabian Baths: Step into the grandeur of these well-preserved public baths, with separate sections for men and women. Explore changing rooms, pools, saunas, and even a palestra (exercise area).

Private Homes

House of the Vettii: Immerse yourself in luxury at this opulent residence adorned with stunning frescoes depicting mythological scenes and daily activities. Marvel at the intricate mosaic floors and imagine the lavish lifestyle of its wealthy owners.

House of the Tragic Poet: This poignant site features a poignant mosaic depicting a mask of comedy and one of tragedy, inspiring its name. Explore the house's various rooms, including a kitchen with preserved food remains.

Bakery: Witness the remnants of a working bakery, complete with its stone mill, ovens, and storage jars. Imagine the aroma of freshly baked bread that once filled the air.

Eerie Reminders

Casts of Victims: These haunting sculptures, created by the ash filling victims' bodies, offer a stark reminder of the eruption's devastating impact. Imagine their final moments and the tragedy that unfolded.

Garden of the Fugitives: This poignant site showcases the remains of 13 people who sought refuge under a shelter, only to be tragically killed by the volcanic ash. Reflect on the fragility of life and the power of nature.

Beyond the Ruins

Antiquarium: Enhance your understanding with exhibits showcasing artifacts unearthed from

Pompeii, including household items, tools, and religious objects.

National Archaeological Museum of Naples: Explore a vast collection of Pompeian treasures, including frescoes, sculptures, and everyday objects, providing a deeper historical context.

Tips for Your Visit

- Wear comfortable shoes for uneven terrain.
- Purchase tickets in advance, especially during peak season.
- Consider a guided tour for deeper insights and historical context.
- Bring sunscreen, a hat, and water, as shade is limited.
- Respect the site and artifacts, and avoid touching or removing anything.

Remember, Pompeii is a journey through time, a place where history whispers secrets and imagination paints vivid pictures. By immersing yourself in the archaeological details, you'll gain a profound appreciation for the lives lived, lost, and forever preserved in this captivating ancient city.

History and significance

Pompeii, Italy, isn't just a collection of stone structures, it's a poignant story frozen in volcanic ash. Its history and significance stretch beyond the tragedy of its eruption, offering a window into Roman life, a captivating example of urban planning, and a powerful reminder of nature's immense power.

A Snapshot of Roman Life

Imagine vibrant shops lining cobbled streets, bustling marketplaces filled with merchants and shoppers, and grand public spaces echoing with laughter and conversation. Pompeii, in 79 AD, was a thriving Roman city with a diverse population, each carrying on their daily lives – bakers kneading dough, children playing games, priests performing rituals. The eruption tragically preserved everything, offering a unique glimpse into their homes, businesses, and everyday routines.

An Urban Planning Marvel

Beyond the individual stories, Pompeii showcases sophisticated Roman engineering and innovative city planning. Explore the intricate network of underground aqueducts that supplied fresh water, marvel at the efficient drainage system, and witness the well-organized layout of residential and public areas. Pompeii serves as a testament to the advanced urban planning capabilities of the Roman Empire.

A Stark Reminder of Nature's Power

The tragedy of Pompeii lies not just in the lives lost but also in the stark reminder of nature's unyielding force. Mount Vesuvius, once a seemingly peaceful mountain, transformed into a destructive force, burying the city under ash and pumice. The haunting casts of victims, their expressions forever etched in agony, serve as a powerful reminder of nature's unpredictable power and the fragility of human existence.

The Significance for You

Visiting Pompeii isn't just about witnessing ruins, it's about

- **Connecting with the past:** Imagine the lives lived, the laughter shared, and the tragedies endured, gaining a deeper understanding of Roman society and daily life.

- **Appreciating urban planning:** Witness the ingenuity and sophistication of Roman engineering, offering valuable insights into urban development even today.

- **Reflecting on nature's power:** Confront the destructive force of nature and our vulnerability to its whims, fostering a sense of respect and caution.

Pompeii isn't just a tourist destination, it's a living museum, a teacher of history, and a poignant reminder of our place in the world. Let your visit be a journey through time, sparking your imagination and leaving you with a deeper appreciation for the past, the present, and the enduring power of human stories.

Tips for visiting and guided tours

Pompeii, Italy, offers a unique journey through time, but planning is crucial for making the most of your visit. Here are some essential tips and insights on guided tours to enhance your experience.

Essential Tips

Tickets and Timing: Buy tickets online in advance, especially during peak season. Consider arriving early to beat the crowds. The site opens at 9:00 AM.

Comfortable Gear: Wear sturdy shoes for uneven terrain and sun protection (hat, sunscreen, sunglasses) as shade is limited.

Hydration and Snacks: Bring water and consider packing light snacks, as few food options are available within the ruins.

Respectful Exploration: Stick to designated paths, don't touch artifacts, and be mindful of preserving this historical treasure.

Accessibility: Most areas are accessible, but some require navigating steps or uneven paths. Ask about wheelchair accessibility if needed.

Guided Tours

Deeper Insights: Hiring a knowledgeable guide unlocks hidden stories, historical context, and fascinating details you might miss otherwise.

Variety of Options: Choose from group tours offering a general overview to private tours tailored to your interests and pace.

Language Preference: Opt for tours in your preferred language to ensure you fully grasp the historical significance and details.

Booking in Advance: Secure your tour spot beforehand, especially during peak season, to avoid disappointment.

Popular Tour Options

Standard Overview Tours: Provide a comprehensive introduction to Pompeii's history, layout, and key structures.

Thematic Tours: Focus on specific aspects like daily life, architecture, religion, or the eruption itself.

Family-Friendly Tours: Engage children with interactive activities and storytelling methods, making history fun and accessible.

Night Tours: Offer a unique atmosphere and insights into the city's mysterious past (availability may vary).

Additional Tips:
- **Combine with Naples:** Explore nearby Naples before or after visiting Pompeii for a richer cultural experience.

- **Visit the Antiquarium:** This on-site museum showcases artifacts unearthed from the city, enriching your understanding.
- **Download an Audio Guide:** If opting for self-guided exploration, consider an audio guide for additional information and commentary.
- **Respect Local Vendors:** While outside the site, be mindful of local vendors and negotiate politely if interested in their souvenirs.

By following these tips and considering guided tours, you can ensure a rewarding and informative visit to Pompeii. Remember, respect the site, embrace the learning experience, and let your imagination paint vivid pictures of the lives once lived in this extraordinary ancient city.

CHAPTER 11

Sorrento

Sorrento, a captivating town perched on the cliffs overlooking the azure waters of the Tyrrhenian Sea, isn't just a popular tourist destination, it's a treasure trove of charm, history, and breathtaking beauty. From wandering through labyrinthine streets adorned with vibrant flowers to savoring delectable cuisine and soaking in panoramic views, Sorrento promises an unforgettable Italian experience.

Immerse Yourself in History and Culture

Old Town Charm: Get lost in the heart of Sorrento, exploring the maze-like alleys of the historic center. Discover hidden piazzas, admire centuries-old buildings adorned with colorful balconies, and stumble upon artisan workshops showcasing local craftsmanship.

Museo Correale: Delve into the region's rich tapestry at the Museo Correale, housing an impressive collection of archaeological artifacts, paintings, and decorative arts.

Duomo: Witness the grandeur of the Sorrento Cathedral, showcasing a harmonious blend of Romanesque and Baroque architectural styles. Step inside to admire the intricately painted ceilings and stunning altarpieces.

Indulge in Culinary Delights

Lemons Take Center Stage: Savor the unique flavors of Sorrento lemons, a local specialty used in everything from refreshing drinks and zesty pastas to fragrant Limoncello, a must-try liqueur.

Fresh Seafood Delights: Treat your taste buds to the freshest seafood, from succulent pasta dishes like spaghetti alle vongole (clams) to grilled octopus and local fish specialties.

Pizza Perfection: While not technically Neapolitan pizza, Sorrentine pizzas offer a distinct yet equally delicious experience. Enjoy thin-crust pizzas topped with local ingredients like mozzarella di bufala and fresh herbs.

Sweet Endings: Don't miss out on the tempting pastries and desserts, like the ricotta-filled delizia al limone or the classic babà soaked in rum.

Embrace the Panoramic Beauty

Cliffside Views: Take a leisurely stroll along the scenic Via Tasso, lined with shops and cafes, and be mesmerized by the breathtaking vistas of the coastline and Mount Vesuvius in the distance.

Centro Storico: The beating heart of Sorrento, this labyrinthine maze of narrow streets, piazzas, and artisan shops offers a glimpse into the town's traditional charm. Get lost in the winding alleys, discover hidden churches, and savor the local atmosphere.

Marina Grande: Descend to the charming Marina Grande, the old fishermen's quarter, and soak up the vibrant atmosphere. Enjoy boat tours exploring hidden coves and iconic rock formations along the Amalfi Coast.

Seiano: Nestled on a cliff overlooking the sea, Seiano offers a quieter ambiance and stunning panoramic views. Wander through the citrus groves, relax on the beach, and visit the charming Sant'Anna Church.

Gardens of Villa Comunale: Wander through the serene gardens of Villa Comunale, offering panoramic views, fragrant flower beds, and a tranquil escape from the bustling town center.

Cloister of San Francesco: Step back in time at the 14th-century Cloister of San Francesco, featuring a peaceful cloister garden and charming frescoes.

Beyond the Town

Capri Getaway: Embark on a day trip to the glamorous island of Capri, reachable by ferry from Sorrento. Explore the vibrant Piazzetta, discover hidden coves, and marvel at the natural wonder of the Blue Grotto.

Amalfi Coast Adventure: Take a scenic boat tour or bus ride along the Amalfi Coast, discovering charming villages like Positano and Amalfi, nestled amidst dramatic cliffs and turquoise waters.

Planning Your Sorrento Escape

When to Visit: Spring (April-June) and autumn (September-October) offer pleasant weather and fewer crowds. July and August are peak season, with higher prices and larger crowds.

Getting Around: The town center is walkable, but buses and taxis are available for exploring further areas.

Accommodation: Choose from a variety of hotels, guesthouses, and apartments to suit your budget and preferences. Sorrento awaits with its captivating charm, rich history, and endless beauty.

CHAPTER 12

Beyond the Amalfi Coast

As enchanting as the Amalfi Coast may be, Campania, the region that cradles it, boasts a treasure trove of experiences waiting to be discovered. From ancient ruins whispering tales of forgotten empires to vibrant cities pulsating with life, and from volcanic landscapes offering dramatic backdrops to hidden villages exuding timeless charm, each corner promises an unforgettable adventure. So, lace up your walking shoes, broaden your horizons, and embark on a journey beyond the Amalfi Coast!

Venturing Inland:

Pompeii & Herculaneum: Explore remarkably preserved homes, streets, and public spaces, and imagine the lives of their inhabitants before the fateful day.

Valley of Temples: Journey to Paestum, where majestic Greek temples stand proudly amid rolling hills. Immerse yourself in the history of Magna Graecia and marvel at the architectural feats of a bygone era.

Royal Majesty in Caserta: Witness the grandeur of the Royal Palace of Caserta, a UNESCO World Heritage Site and one of the largest royal palaces in the world. Be mesmerized by its opulent chambers, sprawling gardens, and stunning park.

Medieval Hill Towns: Discover the charm of hill towns like Ravello, perched on cliffs overlooking the Amalfi Coast, or wander through the historic center of Salerno, adorned with medieval architecture and a vibrant university atmosphere.

Nature's Embrace
Diverse Landscapes: From the towering peaks of the Cervati Mountains to the rolling hills dotted with vineyards and olive groves, Cilento National

Park boasts a variety of landscapes. Explore hidden coves along the dramatic coastline, delve into verdant gorges carved by rivers, and witness breathtaking panoramic views from mountain summits.

Mount Vesuvius: Hike to the crater of Europe's only active volcano and peer into the depths of its power. Witness the awe-inspiring landscapes shaped by volcanic activity and learn about the region's geological history.

Cilento National Park: Immerse yourself in the diverse landscapes of Cilento National Park, encompassing rugged coastlines, lush forests, and charming villages. Hike through scenic trails, explore hidden coves, and discover the park's rich biodiversity.

Island Escapes: Embark on a day trip to the islands of Capri or Ischia, each offering unique experiences. Explore Capri's glamorous piazzas, discover the Blue Grotto's mystical beauty, or relax on Ischia's thermal beaches and charming villages.

Culinary Delights

Neapolitan Pizza Perfection: Savor the original Neapolitan pizza, made with simple, fresh ingredients and cooked in wood-fired ovens. Explore iconic pizzerias in Naples and indulge in the city's culinary soul.

Beyond Pizza: Campania's cuisine extends far beyond pizza. From fresh seafood dishes along the coast to flavorful pasta creations and rich cheeses, tantalize your taste buds with regional specialties.

Wine Appreciation: Explore the region's renowned wine-producing areas like Falerno del Sannio or Vesuvio. Embark on winery tours, sample local varietals, and discover the unique flavors influenced by volcanic soil and Mediterranean sunshine.

Experiences Beyond the Tourist Trail

Cooking Classes: Learn the secrets of Neapolitan cuisine by participating in a hands-on cooking class. Master the art of pizza making, prepare traditional pasta dishes, and gain insights into local culinary traditions.

Limoncello Making: Discover the secrets behind the iconic liqueur in a limoncello-making workshop. Learn about the production process, using fresh Sorrento lemons, and savor the sweet and refreshing taste of your creation.

Local Festivals: Immerse yourself in the vibrant culture by attending a local festival. From traditional music and dance performances to food fairs and religious processions, experience the heart and soul of Campania's communities.

Planning Your Campania Adventure

Consider the season: Spring (April-June) and autumn (September-October) offer pleasant weather and fewer crowds. July and August are peak season, with higher prices and larger crowds.

Explore public transportation: Buses and trains connect major cities and towns, making it easy to navigate the region. Consider purchasing a Campania Artecard for discounted entry to attractions and public transportation savings.

Choose your base: Decide between a bustling city like Naples or a charming coastal town like Sorrento or Salerno as your base, depending on your desired pace and interests.

Paestum: Ancient Greek Temples

Step beyond the vibrant Amalfi Coast and into a realm of whispers from antiquity. Paestum, bathed in the warm Italian sun and kissed by the Tyrrhenian Sea, unveils three majestic Doric temples, remnants of a once-thriving Greek city named Poseidonia. These colossal structures, remarkably preserved, transport you back centuries, painting vivid pictures of a past where gods and mortals walked hand-in-hand.

A Journey Through Time

Temples of Grandeur: Stand in awe before the Basilica (Temple of Hera I), the oldest in mainland Italy, dating back to 550 BC. Marvel at its 50 Doric columns, towering nearly 13 meters high, each a silent testament to ancient engineering prowess.

Temple of Neptune: Explore the second largest temple, dedicated to Poseidon or Neptune, the god of the sea. Built around 450 BC, its 36 fluted columns and well-preserved pediment details transport you to a bygone era of myths and legends.

Temple of Athena or Ceres: Discover the smallest of the three, believed to be dedicated either to Athena, goddess of wisdom, or Ceres, goddess of agriculture. Its graceful proportions and intricate details offer a glimpse into the evolution of Doric architecture.

Beyond the Temples

Museum Unveils Treasures: Delve deeper into the city's history at the National Archaeological Museum. Explore a treasure trove of artifacts, including sculptures, frescoes, and everyday objects, providing a fascinating glimpse into daily life in ancient Poseidonia.

Walking Through History: Stroll along the Sacred Way, an ancient road lined with remnants of temples, shrines, and public buildings. Imagine chariot processions and bustling crowds once filling this space, bringing the past to life.

Amphitheater Echoes of Performances: Step into the ancient amphitheater, built in the 2nd century BC. Imagine the drama unfolding on stage, from gladiatorial combats to theatrical performances, echoing through the centuries.

An Escape Beyond the Ordinary

Nature's Serenity: Embrace the natural beauty surrounding the archaeological site. Wander through olive groves, soak up the sunshine on the nearby beach, or enjoy a picnic amidst the ruins, creating memories that transcend time.

Culinary Delights: Savor the flavors of southern Italy in local restaurants. Indulge in fresh seafood dishes, savor local cheeses and olives, and finish with a sweet treat like sfogliatella, a flaky pastry filled with ricotta cream.

Beyond Paestum: Explore the vibrant city of Salerno, with its medieval architecture and lively university atmosphere, or journey to Pompeii and Herculaneum to witness the haunting beauty of these ancient Roman cities frozen in time.

Planning Your Paestum Adventure

Seasons: Spring (April-June) and autumn (September-October) offer pleasant weather and fewer crowds. July and August are peak season, with higher prices and larger crowds.

Getting There: Easily accessible by train or bus from Naples and Salerno. Buses connect nearby towns, offering flexibility.

Accommodation: Choose from charming guesthouses, hotels, or farm stays in Paestum or nearby towns, depending on your budget and desired experience.

Paestum is not just about magnificent temples, it's about experiencing history, immersing yourself in nature, and creating lasting memories. So, pack your sense of adventure, unleash your inner historian, and allow the whispers of the past to guide you on an unforgettable journey to Paestum!

Salerno: Medieval History & Modern Vibe

Beyond the Amalfi Coast's captivating beauty lies Salerno, a vibrant city boasting a rich history interwoven with a modern pulse. Explore enchanting medieval alleyways, wander past centuries-old churches, and soak up the lively university atmosphere. From historical treasures to bustling piazzas and contemporary art, Salerno offers an enthralling blend of the past and present, ensuring an unforgettable Italian experience.

Embrace the Medieval Spirit

Wander Through Time: Lose yourself in the heart of Salerno's historic center, a labyrinth of narrow streets lined with pastel-colored buildings. Discover hidden piazzas, admire architectural gems like the 12th-century Duomo, and marvel at the medieval fortress of Arechi, perched on a hilltop overlooking the city.

Museo Diocesano: Step back in time at the Museo Diocesano, housing an impressive collection of religious art, including medieval sculptures, paintings, and manuscripts. Admire the intricate details and delve into the city's spiritual heritage.

Longobard Spuren: Unearth the legacy of the Lombards, who ruled Salerno from the 8th to the 11th centuries. Visit the medieval complex of San Matteo, including the Chiesa di San Pietro a Corte with its Lombard-style arches and intricate sculptures.

Immerse in the Modern Buzz

Lungomare Promenade: Stroll along the scenic Lungomare promenade, a vibrant seaside walkway lined with palm trees and cafes. Enjoy breathtaking views of the Salerno Gulf, watch street performers entertain crowds, and soak up the city's modern energy.

Villa Comunale: Escape the urban buzz and relax in the verdant oasis of Villa Comunale, a public park adorned with sculptures, fountains, and lush gardens. Enjoy a picnic under the shade of trees, people-watch, or join locals for a leisurely stroll.

Teatro Verdi: Immerse yourself in the cultural scene at the Teatro Verdi, a magnificent opera house showcasing a diverse program of performances, from classical operas and ballets to contemporary plays and concerts.

Beyond the City Walls

Vietri sul Mare: Embark on a day trip to the charming village of Vietri sul Mare, renowned for its centuries-old tradition of ceramic craftsmanship. Wander through colorful streets lined with ceramic shops, witness artisans at work, and discover unique treasures to take home.

Amalfi Coast Gems: Explore the picturesque towns of the Amalfi Coast, like Positano with its iconic cliffside houses and vibrant piazzas, or Ravello perched on a hilltop offering breathtaking panoramic views.

Cilento National Park: Immerse yourself in the diverse landscapes of Cilento National Park, encompassing rugged coastlines, lush forests, and charming villages. Hike through scenic trails, explore hidden coves, and discover the park's rich biodiversity.

Savor the Flavors

Fresh Seafood Delights: Indulge in the freshest seafood dishes at waterfront restaurants overlooking the Salernó Gulf. Savor local specialties like pasta with clams, grilled octopus, and frittura mista (fried seafood mix).

Sweet Indulgences: Don't miss Salerno's signature dessert, torrone, a nougat-like candy made with honey, egg whites, and toasted almonds. Explore local pasticcerias and discover other tempting treats like sfogliatella and delizia al limone.

Wine & Dine in Style: Enjoy a romantic dinner in a charming piazza, savor traditional dishes paired with local wines, and experience the warmth of Italian hospitality.

Planning Your Salerno Escape

Seasons: Spring (April-June) and autumn (September-October) offer pleasant weather and fewer crowds. July and August are peak season, with higher prices and larger crowds.

Getting Around: Salerno is easily accessible by train from major Italian cities. Buses connect nearby towns and villages, offering flexibility. Explore the city center on foot or rent a bike for a more active experience.

Accommodation: Choose from a variety of hotels, guesthouses, and apartments to suit your budget and preferences. Opt for a stay in the historic center for easy access to sights, or enjoy the seaside vibe with a Lungomare location.

Caserta: Royal Palace & Gardens

Nestled amidst the rolling hills of Campania, Italy, lies the magnificent Royal Palace of Caserta, a UNESCO World Heritage Site and a testament to the extravagant lifestyle of the Bourbon kings. Often dubbed the "Versailles of Italy" for its sheer scale and opulent interiors, the palace is a must-visit for anyone seeking a glimpse into the grandeur of 18th-century royalty. But Caserta's allure extends far beyond its palatial walls, encompassing sprawling baroque gardens, cascading fountains, and a serene English Garden, offering a delightful escape into nature's embrace.

Step into Royal Opulence

The Grand Staircase: Prepare to be awestruck as you ascend the monumental Grand Staircase, a masterpiece of Baroque architecture adorned with sculptures, frescoes, and intricate marble details. Imagine the grand processions that once graced these steps, adding to the palace's majestic aura.

Royal Apartments: Wander through a series of opulent chambers, each showcasing the exquisite taste and wealth of the Bourbon kings. Be mesmerized by the Throne Room, adorned with rich tapestries and gilded furniture, and the Palatine Chapel, featuring stunning religious artworks and a breathtaking dome.

Theatrical Delights: Immerse yourself in the world of courtly entertainment at the opulent Teatro di Corte. Imagine the grandeur of operas and theatrical performances staged within its richly decorated walls, complete with a royal box for the king and his family.

Explore Verdant Delights
Baroque Gardens: Step outside the palace and be greeted by the sprawling Baroque Gardens, a meticulously designed masterpiece showcasing geometric patterns, manicured lawns, and cascading fountains. Stroll along tree-lined avenues adorned with statues, lose yourself in the labyrinthine

hedges, and capture the grandeur of the palace reflected in the reflecting pools.

Cascading Fountains: Marvel at the intricate network of fountains, each playing a unique melody as water gracefully cascades down various levels. The most impressive is the Great Waterfall, a towering spectacle visible from afar, offering a refreshing contrast to the manicured gardens.

English Garden: Seeking a tranquil escape? Immerse yourself in the serene English Garden, a stark contrast to the formality of the Baroque Gardens. Wander along winding paths amidst lush greenery, discover hidden grottos and sculptures, and enjoy the calming sounds of nature.

Beyond the Palace Walls

Explore Casertavecchia: Perched on a hill overlooking the palace, discover Casertavecchia, the medieval predecessor of modern-day Caserta. Explore its charming streets, visit the 12th-century

Cathedral, and soak up the historical ambiance of this ancient town.

Venture to Naples: Take a day trip to the vibrant city of Naples, known for its rich history, delicious pizza, and archaeological treasures like Pompeii and Herculaneum.

Discover the Amalfi Coast: Immerse yourself in the breathtaking scenery and charming villages of the Amalfi Coast, a short drive away from Caserta.

Planning Your Royal Escape

Seasons: Spring (April-June) and autumn (September-October) offer pleasant weather and fewer crowds. July and August are peak season, with higher prices and larger crowds.

Getting There: Caserta is easily accessible by train from major Italian cities like Naples and Rome. Buses connect nearby towns and villages.

Accommodation: Choose from a variety of hotels, guesthouses, and apartments in Caserta or nearby towns, depending on your budget and desired experience.

Tickets & Tours: Purchase tickets online in advance, especially during peak season, to avoid long queues. Consider joining guided tours for deeper insights into the palace's history and architecture.

With its opulent interiors, meticulously designed gardens, and serene natural spaces, the Royal Palace of Caserta offers an unforgettable experience for history buffs, nature lovers, and anyone seeking a glimpse into royal grandeur.

CHAPTER 13

Useful websites and apps

Navigating the Amalfi Coast can be thrilling, but having the right digital tools can elevate your experience from good to unforgettable. Here are some essential websites and apps to bookmark for your Italian adventure:

Official Information and Planning

Amalfi Coast Tourist Board: (amalficoast.com) The official source for comprehensive information on towns, transportation, events, and activities.

Sorrento Coast DMO: (sorrentotouristoffice.com) Offers details on the Sorrento area, including transportation options and day trips to the Amalfi Coast.

Campania Region - Tourism Portal:

(incampania.com) The official Campania region website, covering major attractions, cultural events, and travel tips.

UnicoCampania: (unicocampania.it)

Provides timetables and ticket information for all public transportation (buses and ferries) across Campania.

Accommodation and Activities

Booking Platforms: Popular options like Booking.com, Expedia, and Airbnb offer a vast selection of hotels, apartments, villas, and B&Bs.

Local Websites: For a more personalized experience, search for smaller accommodations on local websites like Amalfi.com or Positano.com

Local Tour Operators: Look for companies based in specific towns (Amalfi Coast Excursions, Sorrento Day Trips) for unique experiences.

Navigation and Communication

Maps and Apps: Download offline maps like Google Maps or Maps.me for reliable navigation. Consider language translation apps like Google Translate or Reverso for smooth communication.

Public Transportation Apps: Use "UnicoCampania" app for ticket purchases and live bus/ferry tracking. Explore "Moovit" or "Transit" for multi-modal trip planning with public transport and walking directions.

Additional Resources

Ferry Schedules: (directferries.com) - Conveniently compare schedules and prices for various ferry companies operating between Amalfi Coast towns, Capri, and Naples.

Car Rentals: Compare prices and options from international brands (Avis, Hertz) or local companies (Maggiore, Auto Europa).

Weather Forecast: Stay informed with reliable sources like AccuWeather or BBC Weather.

Currency Exchange: Check rates and fees on XE Currency Converter or TransferWise before exchanging money.

Emergency Numbers: Save the Italian emergency number (112) and local police station numbers for your chosen towns.

Bonus Apps

Amalfi Coast S.L. App: Official app of the SITA bus company, offering live timetables, ticket purchases, and route information.

Trenitalia App: Official app for train travel, covering routes and tickets within Italy, including Naples and Salerno.

HelloTalk: Connect with locals for language exchange and cultural insights.

Remember
- Download apps and offline maps before your trip for seamless use without internet access.
- Utilize multiple resources for comparing prices, schedules, and options.
- Don't hesitate to ask locals for recommendations and hidden gems beyond tourist guides.

With these digital tools and open curiosity, your Amalfi Coast adventure is sure to be enriching and unforgettable!

Maps

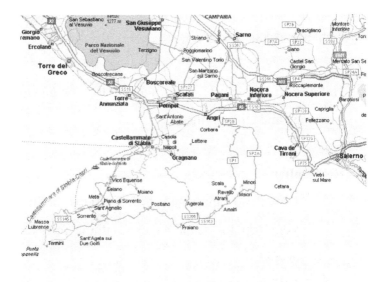

To help you make the most of your trip, here's a guide to essential maps that will keep you oriented and ensure you don't miss a beat:

1. Regional Overview

Amalfi Coast Tourist Map: This map provides a broad overview of the entire region, highlighting major towns and villages, transportation routes, and points of interest. It's a great starting point for planning your itinerary and understanding the lay of the land.

Google Maps: Always a reliable option, Google Maps offers a comprehensive and interactive map of the Amalfi Coast. You can zoom in and out to see specific areas, find directions, and even explore street views.

2. Town Maps

Individual Town Maps: Each major town on the Amalfi Coast, like Positano, Amalfi, and Ravello, has its own detailed map. These maps typically show streets, piazzas, attractions, restaurants, and shops. You can usually find them at tourist information offices or download them online.

3. Hiking Trails

Hiking Trail Maps: If you're planning on hitting the trails, be sure to get a map specifically for the hike you're interested in. These maps will show the route, elevation changes, points of interest, and estimated hiking times. Popular trails like the Path of the Gods and Valle delle Ferriere have dedicated maps available online or at local shops.

4. Transportation Maps

Bus Routes: Public transportation is a great way to get around the Amalfi Coast. Bus route maps are available at bus stops and tourist information offices. They show the different routes, stops, and timetables.

Ferry Routes: If you're planning on taking a ferry to explore hidden coves or neighboring islands like Capri, you'll need a ferry route map. These maps show the different routes, departure and arrival points, and ticket information.

Additional Tips

- **Download Offline Maps:** Before you head out, download offline versions of the maps you need onto your phone or tablet. This will ensure you have access to navigation even without an internet connection.

- Ask Locals: Don't hesitate to ask locals or shopkeepers for directions or recommendations. They often have the best insider knowledge of hidden gems and shortcuts.

By having the right maps at your disposal, you can navigate the Amalfi Coast with confidence and discover all the beauty and charm this incredible region has to offer. Remember, getting lost can sometimes lead to the most unexpected and delightful discoveries, so don't be afraid to wander and explore beyond the map!

Glossary of Italian Terms

Navigating a new country can be challenging, especially when it comes to language. This glossary equips you with essential Italian terms you might encounter during your Amalfi Coast adventure, ensuring a smooth and enjoyable experience.

General
- **Buongiorno:** Good morning (until lunch)
- **Buonasera:** Good evening (after lunch)
- **Grazie:** Thank you
- **Prego:** You're welcome
- **Scusi:** Excuse me
- **Mi scusi:** I apologize
- **Parla inglese?:** Do you speak English?
- **Quanto costa?:** How much does it cost?
- **Dove si trova...?:** Where is...?
- **Posso avere il conto, per favore?:** Can I have the bill, please?

Food & Drinks

- **Menu:** Menu
- **Antipasto:** Starter
- **Primo:** First course (pasta, rice)
- **Secondo:** Main course (meat, fish)
- **Contorno:** Side dish
- **Dolce:** Dessert
- **Acqua:** Water
- **Vino:** Wine
- **Birra:** Beer
- **Caffè:** Coffee
- **Con latte:** With milk
- **Senza:** Without
- **Per favore:** Please

Transportation

- **Taxi:** Taxi
- **Autobus:** Bus
- **Treno:** Train
- **Biglietto:** Ticket
- **Stazione:** Station
- **Fermata:** Stop

- **Prossima fermata:** Next stop
- **Biglietto singolo/andata e ritorno:** One-way/round-trip ticket
- **Quanto tempo ci vuole?:** How long does it take?

Shopping
- **Negozio:** Shop
- **Quanto costa questo?:** How much does this cost?
- **Posso provarlo?:** Can I try it on?
- **Posso avere uno sconto?:** Can I have a discount?
- **Carte di credito accettate?:** Do you accept credit cards?
- **Posso pagare con carta?:** Can I pay with a card?

Beaches & Activities
- **Spiaggia:** Beach
- **Ombrello:** Umbrella
- **Lettino:** Lounger

- **Mare:** Sea
- **Spiaggia libera:** Public beach
- **Escursione:** Excursion
- **Museo:** Museum
- **Chiesa:** Church
- **Castello:** Castle
- **Ingresso:** Entrance
- **Orario di apertura:** Opening hours

Additional Phrases

- **Buona giornata!:** Have a good day!
- **Buona sera!:** Have a good evening!
- **Buon appetito!:** Enjoy your meal!
- **Arrivederci!:** Goodbye!
- **Mi piace:** I like it.
- **Non capisco:** I don't understand.
- **Può parlare più lentamente?:** Can you speak slower?
- **Posso aiutarti?:** Can I help you?

Remember

- Pronunciation is key! Many Italian words have silent letters and accented syllables. Listen carefully and repeat after locals when possible.

- Don't be afraid to make mistakes! Italians appreciate attempts to speak their language and are usually happy to help.

- Enjoy the journey! Learning a few basic Italian phrases will enhance your experience and connect you with the local culture.

CONCLUSION

As you close the pages of this travel guide, I hope you're filled with anticipation, excitement, and a deeper understanding of the breathtaking Amalfi Coast and its enchanting destinations like Capri, Naples, and Pompeii.

With its azure waters, charming villages, and rich history, the Amalfi Coast offers a tapestry of experiences that will leave an indelible mark on your heart. From the stunning vistas of Capri to the ancient ruins of Pompeii, the coast invites you to explore its every corner.

Indulge in the region's culinary delights, from freshly caught seafood to the flavorful dishes of Naples. Every meal along the Amalfi Coast is a celebration of Italian culture and a journey of taste. But it's not just the beauty of the Amalfi Coast that captivates, it's the warmth and hospitality of its people. Engage with locals, exchange smiles and greetings in Italian, and you'll discover that the

Amalfi Coast's heart is as welcoming as its landscapes are breathtaking.

As you embark on your adventure, don't forget to capture the moments that take your breath away. Let your camera and journal be your companions, preserving the beauty, flavors, and emotions of this incredible journey.

Remember, a well-prepared trip is a more enjoyable one. From packing essentials to understanding local customs, this guide has equipped you with the knowledge you need to navigate the Amalfi Coast with confidence. The Amalfi Coast is not just a destination, it's a story waiting to be written. It's a place where sunsets paint the sky in hues of gold and crimson, where the sea whispers tales of ancient civilizations, and where every alleyway holds the promise of discovery. As you bid farewell to the Amalfi Coast, know that the memories you've created here will stay with you forever. Whether you've explored hidden coves, marveled at panoramic views, or delved into ancient history, the Amalfi Coast has left its mark on your soul.

While this guide may end here, your journey through the Amalfi Coast continues. May the memories you've collected on this coast be a source of joy and inspiration for years to come. And, when the time is right, may you return to the Amalfi Coast to create new stories, explore new horizons, and bask in the eternal beauty of this Italian paradise.

The Amalfi Coast is more than a destination, it's an invitation to explore, a canvas for your adventures, and a place where every moment is a cherished memory. Until we meet again in this enchanting corner of the world, remember that the spirit of the Amalfi Coast is always with you, wherever your travels may take you next. Buon viaggio! - Safe travels!

Made in United States
Orlando, FL
30 December 2024

56694994R00147